THE FAMILY FORMULA

Protecting Your Family's Hair-Care Legacy

RUBEN ALCOBA, ESQ.

ALCOBA LAW GROUP, P.A.
Doral, Florida

THE FAMILY FORMULA

Protecting Your Family's Hair-Care Legacy

This is a work of fiction. Names, characters, businesses, companies, organizations, products, places, events, and incidents are either the products of the author's imagination or are used fictitiously. Any resemblance to actual persons, living or dead, or to actual companies, products, events, or locales is entirely coincidental.

Legal Disclaimer. This book is intended for general educational and informational purposes only. It does not constitute legal, tax, financial, regulatory, or other professional advice, and it is not a substitute for the advice of a qualified attorney or other licensed professional in your jurisdiction. Reading this book does not create an attorney-client relationship with the author, with Alcoba Law Group, P.A., or with any of its attorneys. Laws vary by jurisdiction and change over time, and the outcome of any matter depends on its specific facts, timing, evidence, and professional judgment. Before acting, or refraining from acting, on the basis of anything contained in this book, consult a qualified professional regarding your particular situation. The author and publisher expressly disclaim all liability for any loss or damage arising directly or indirectly from the use of, or reliance upon, the contents of this book.

Published by Alcoba Law Group, P.A.
7791 NW 46 Street, Suite 218
Doral, Florida 33166
www.alcobalaw.com

ISBN: 979-8-9945872-8-7
First Edition, 2026
Printed in the United States of America

To Alexa, and to every family that carried a formula across a border without knowing it was an inheritance.

Table of Contents

INTRODUCTION
The Inheritance Nobody Claimed

I wrote this book for my niece Alexa, who spent a summer at the front desk of my law office, and for whom I wanted to do more than hand out assignments. I wanted to show her what I do, and why, in a way that would keep her turning pages while it taught her what life in this practice is actually about.

The first lesson is the simplest and the hardest: nothing is ever perfect, and the only thing required to finish anything is to start it.

The second is what a law office looks like when it truly values its clients. We listen to the whole story before we touch a single document. We recommend only what is right and ethical. And then we step back and let the client choose the road, because the road belongs to them, not to us. I also wanted her to learn the counsel nobody expects from a lawyer: that silence is sometimes the answer, that not acting is sometimes the best course of action, and that time, in the end, is the master of all our destinies.

The third lesson is about the torch. We are immigrants. My mother is passing hers to us now, and that obliges us to pass one on in turn. But not every torch is worth carrying. A legacy built only of assets is finite; it burns down to whatever it was worth on the day it changed hands. A legacy built of knowledge, judgment, and possibility keeps lighting new fires long after the people who carried it are gone. That is the inheritance worth leaving, and it is the one this book is about.

The last lesson is the one that governs the rest: what matters is what we do for our fellow man. Life will determine the rewards.

So, while this book was written for Alexa, it was written for my whole family, and for every family like ours. Success almost always takes longer than you expect. Do not quit. If you keep going, time will hand you something worth passing on, a legacy full of possibilities instead of one void of them.

The families in these pages are inventions. The lessons are not.

Everything that follows asks only one thing of you, and it is the same thing I asked of Alexa on her first morning: you do not have to be ready, and it does not have to be perfect.

All you have to do is start.

PART I
THE INHERITANCE

CHAPTER ONE
The Amber Bottle

The bottle was the color of dark honey, and the woman who set it on my desk apologized for it.

"*Es solo una receta de mi mamá*," she said. It is only a recipe of my mother's. She smoothed the front of her blouse with both hands, in the way of a person who is about to ask for something she believes she has no right to ask for. "I am sorry to take your time with this, *Licenciado*."

Her name was María Restrepo. She was fifty-four years old, born in Medellín, and she had lived in this country for eleven years. I knew this because my office manager had taken it down when she called to make the appointment, along with the reason for her visit, which María had stated in six words: "Somebody wants to buy my recipe."

The bottle had no label. A strip of masking tape ran across the front, and on the tape, in careful blue ballpoint, someone had written a single word: FORTALECEDOR. The word means strengthener. Beneath it was the letter M. The M, I would learn, stood for Marta, her mother, who had written that word on ten thousand pieces of tape before her hands gave out, and whose own mother had made the same preparation on a wood stove in a mountain town in Antioquia whose name María still could not say without touching her chest.

My niece was at the front desk that morning, twenty feet and one open door away, pretending to reorganize a filing cabinet that my office manager had organized perfectly in 2019.

Alexa was twenty years old that summer, and she worked in my office five days a week as the result of a negotiation with her mother that neither of them would fully describe to me. What I knew was this: she had finished two years of college, had announced that she was not returning for a third, and had defended the decision with a sentence I had been turning over in my mind for weeks. "College is a subscription service," she told the family table, "for information that is free." Her mother had then looked at me the way my sister has looked at me since we were children. The look means one thing: fix this. So, Alexa answered my phones, ran my copier, and signed the same confidentiality agreement that every employee of the firm signs, because a law office keeps other people's secrets for a living, and even the boss's niece is not an exception. She took notes that she never showed anyone. She watched my clients cross the lobby the way a card player watches a table. On her first day, she informed me that she was there to determine whether what I did was real or whether it was, in her words, "paperwork with a costume on."

That morning, when she saw María's name in the appointment book, she asked if she could sit in.

"No," I said.

"I'll be quiet."

"It is not about quiet. What Mrs. Restrepo tells me in that room is protected. It stays protected because the conversation is between a client and her lawyer, and no one else. Put a third person in the corner, and one of two things happens. Either the client says less than she needs to say, or the law may later decide that the conversation was never private at all. She loses something either way, and she is not coming here to lose things." I picked up my legal pad. "Leave the door open when you bring the coffee. Whatever you happen to hear while doing your job, you keep the way the vault keeps it. That is the arrangement, and it is not negotiable."

She saluted me with two fingers, which is not a gesture of surrender, and went back to the filing cabinet.

* *

María sat down across from me and placed a folder on the desk beside the bottle. Then she moved the bottle an inch to the left, so that it would not be in my way.

"Tell me about it," I said.

"The recipe?"

"Start before the recipe. Tell me about the bottle."

People will hand you a contract in the first minute if you allow it. The contract is never the beginning of the story, and a lawyer who reads it before he knows the story will read it wrong. So, she told me the story. Her grandmother had made the strengthener for the women of her town. Her mother had made it in Medellín, for the neighbors and for the salon on the corner. María had made it here, in the kitchen of her apartment: first for her cousins, then for the women at her church, and then for the two salons in her neighborhood whose owners now bought it by the case. She told me about the customer who shipped six bottles to her sister in Queens every month, about the sister who now had customers of her own, and about the woman who had carried four bottles in a suitcase back to Barranquilla because, she said, you could not find anything like it there, in the very country it came from.

"How long have you been selling it here?"

She counted on her fingers, and she was embarrassed to be counting. "Nine years. Since my second year in Miami. But not selling like a business," she added quickly. "Selling like a neighbor."

Through the open door, I heard the filing cabinet go quiet.

"How many bottles in a good month?"

"Now, with the salons? A hundred and forty. Maybe a hundred and sixty in December."

"At what price?"

"Fourteen dollars. Twelve for the salons."

In the outer office, very faintly, a pen began to move across paper.

"Señora Restrepo, before we open the folder, tell me one more thing. Who knows how to make it? The complete preparation, from start to finish."

"I do. My daughter, Camila, knows most of it. Not the part with the..." She stopped herself, and her hand rose as if to hold the next word inside her mouth. She had almost told me. Eleven years in this country, ten minutes in a lawyer's office, and the thing that three generations of women had kept in their heads had nearly come out as a courtesy, because I had asked a question in a kind voice and she did not want to be difficult.

"Do not tell me," I said. "Not today, and perhaps not ever. I do not need the recipe in order to help you. I need to know who has it."

"I have it. Camila has most of it. And Luz, my *comadre*, helps me on the big days, when the salons order together. She knows the steps, but not the amounts." A sudden worry crossed her face. "Is that bad, that Luz knows?"

"Has Luz ever signed anything? A paper promising to keep it to herself?"

María laughed, a quick, startled laugh, and then she covered her mouth. "Signed? *Licenciado*, she is my *comadre*. She was at Camila's baptism."

I nodded, and I did not say what I was thinking. I have spent twenty years watching what love does when it is asked to work without paper. It is not that love fails; it usually does not. It is that when love fails, it fails completely, and everything that was protected only by love goes down with it. That conversation could wait for another day. Today, there was a folder on my desk.

"Now," I said. "Show me."

* *

The offer was four pages long. Whoever drafted it had been paid to make it look simple.

The buyer was a man named Osvaldo, a distributor who supplied beauty products to salons across three counties and who had been buying the strengthener from María, at wholesale, for two years. He was, she wanted me to understand, a good man. He paid on time. He had sent flowers when her mother passed away. Two weeks earlier, he had taken her to lunch, told her that her product was the finest thing he carried, and slid this folder across the table with a check clipped to the first page. She had not cashed the check. She had also, she admitted, not fully read the folder. It was in English, and it was long, and Osvaldo had explained what it said.

"What did he tell you it said?"

"That he buys the recipe. Forty thousand dollars. Twenty now, and twenty when I teach his laboratory to make it." She said the number the way people say numbers larger than any check they have ever held. Then she said the sentence she had prepared on the drive over, the sentence that was the true reason she had come: "*Licenciado*, I only want to know if it is legal. If the paper is correct. I do not want problems later."

I read it twice. It was correct. That was the problem. It was a correctly drafted purchase of everything.

Paragraph two conveyed the formula, the process, and all related know-how. Paragraph three conveyed all improvements, past and future, which meant that if María ever made the product better, the better version would already belong to Osvaldo. Paragraph five conveyed all intellectual property rights of any kind, registered or unregistered, existing or later arising. Paragraph seven granted him the right to use the names "María" and "Doña María," together with her image and her family's story, in his marketing, forever and worldwide. In paragraph nine, María promised not to make, sell, or help anyone else make a competing hair product for eight years, anywhere the buyer did business. In paragraph ten, María agreed to maintain the confidentiality of the formula for the buyer's benefit. The secret her grandmother had kept would go on being kept, except that it would now be kept for someone else, by contract, by the same woman who used to own it.

I set the pages down and looked at the bottle with the masking tape. I have sat across from this transaction many times in my career, and once or twice in my own life I have been the person on the other side of the desk. I accepted less than something was worth because the money was certain and the worth was not, and I have signed papers that I should have read first. Those are stories for later chapters. But you should know, before you accept any advice from me, that none of it comes from a man who was born knowing better.

"Señora," I said, "the paper is legal. It is well made. If you sign it, it will do exactly what it was built to do."

She let out a breath. "Ah. Good."

"What it was built to do," I said, "is buy a nine-year-old business, its product, its future improvements, your mother's name, and your silence, for forty thousand dollars."

The office was quiet. Somewhere down the hall, the copier was running.

"It is not a business," María said at last, softly, and her hands returned to the hem of her blouse. "*Es solo una receta.*"

* *

What I asked María to do that week, I will set down plainly, because it is the same thing I would ask of you, and it requires no lawyer, no fee, and no filing.

I asked her for four pages, handwritten, in whichever language they arrived.

Page one would describe what makes the product different, in categories only, never the recipe itself. Is it an ingredient? A source? A step in the process, timing, temperature? She was not to write the secret down. She was to write down that a secret exists, and what kind of secret it is, so that she could begin to see it the way the law sees it: not as a memory of her mother, but as a thing, as property, as an asset that three generations of women had built and carried across a border in their heads, paying no duty and declaring nothing, because no one, including them, had ever thought to call it valuable.

Page two would list every person who knows any part of it. Family counts. *Comadres* count. The daughter in the kitchen counts. Next to each name would go one more note: has this person ever signed anything? I told her what the finished page would look like, because it looks the same for nearly every family I have ever sat with. It is a short list of names, bound together by blood, baptism, and thirty years of Sunday dinners, beside a column of signatures that is empty from top to bottom. That empty column is not proof that a family is careless. It is proof that a family is a family. But the law does not read love. The law reads paper, and soon, though not today, we would need to talk about what it costs to introduce paper into a house that has never needed it.

Page three would tell the honest history of her sales: when she first sold a bottle in this country, to whom, through what channels, roughly how many, and at roughly what price. I told her not to clean the history up, and not to leave out the cash sales, the church sales, or the cases that went to Queens. The clean version would be useless to me. Certain doors in the law open or close according to what has already happened, and only true history could tell us which doors we were standing in front of. She asked me which doors. I told her that this was next week's conversation; that there were four of them; and that the folder on my desk was Osvaldo's attempt to buy the contents of all four before she learned they existed.

The fourth thing was not a page. The fourth thing was a full stop. Beginning that afternoon, there would be no more tours of her kitchen for anyone who bought wholesale, no more samples mailed with friendly notes about how the product is made, and no more almost telling an ingredient to a lawyer because he asked in a kind voice. Curiosity is not a reason. From that day forward, the only person who would hear anything about the inside of that bottle would be a person who had signed a paper first. We did not yet have the paper, and that was fine, because the fastest way to protect a secret is simply to close your mouth around it, and closing your mouth costs nothing.

María wrote all of it in a small spiral notebook, nodding as she wrote, and when she finished, she looked up and asked the question that the entire meeting had been walking toward, the question I had been waiting for since she apologized for the bottle.

"*Licenciado*, be honest with me. It is not patented. It is not registered anywhere. There is no paper, no stamp, nothing with a seal. Does it really count as anything, legally?"

"Señora," I said, "the most famous formula in the world is not patented. It has never been. It sits in a vault in Atlanta, and the company that owns it decided more than a century ago that it would rather keep the secret forever than trade it to the government for twenty years of protection and a public filing that anyone could read. The law protects that formula anyway. It protects it not because of a stamp, but because the formula is valuable, because it is secret, and because the company treats it like a secret, with locks, contracts, and closed mouths. That is the entire test. There is no form to file with and no fee to pay. Your formula is smaller. The law it lives under is the same. It counted as property before you walked in here this morning. What it has never had"—and here I picked up Osvaldo's folder and handed it back to her—"is an owner who knew she was an owner. That is the only paper missing, and it is not filed in any office. Señora, with respect: you have a supplier, a customer list, nine years of sales, repeat buyers on two continents, and a competitor attempting to acquire you. You did not walk in here with a recipe. You walked in with a company. It is eleven years old, and no one has ever said its name out loud, including you."

María looked at the bottle for a long moment. Then she did something I did not expect. She reached out, peeled the strip of masking tape from the glass, smoothed it onto the first page of her spiral notebook, and pressed it down with her thumb, the way a person presses something she intends to keep.

The bottle itself she left on my desk.

"So that you remember what we are working on," she said.

* *

Alexa gave María her full smile on the way out and walked her to the elevator. Then she appeared in my doorway holding the legal pad from the front desk. She did not ask permission to come in. She held the pad up so that I could see the arithmetic on it: three numbers overheard through an open door, multiplied.

"A hundred and fifty bottles a month at thirteen dollars and change," she said. "Call it twenty-three or twenty-four thousand a year, and growing, and that is only what she admits to. Nine years of that." She dropped into the chair María had just left. "And somebody offered her forty for the whole thing?"

"You were listening."

"I was doing my job near a door you told me to leave open. There is a difference." She tapped the pad. "Here is my real question, and I want a real answer, not a lawyer's answer. Why shouldn't she take it? Forty thousand dollars, guaranteed, today. Whatever you think the recipe is worth is a theory. The check is not a theory. People like us do not get a lot of checks."

She said *people like us*, and she said it looking at the amber bottle.

"That is a fair argument," I said, because it was. "Certain money has a value that uncertain money does not, and anyone who tells you otherwise has never been poor. If she hears everything I have to say and still wants to sell, I will negotiate the sale myself, and I will sleep fine. Selling is not the mistake."

"Then what is?"

"Selling blind. Think about what you heard this morning. She came in asking whether the paper was legal. That was the only question she believed she was permitted to ask. Not what it is worth. Not what exactly am I giving up. Not why does a man who moves product through three counties want my kitchen recipe badly enough to bring a check to lunch. A distributor is a businessman, Alexa. He does not pay for sentiment. Somewhere in his numbers, that recipe earns his money back and then keeps earning. His offer is not a favor. It is an appraisal. It is the first professional appraisal that formula has ever received, and it arrived at a number he chose, on a form he drafted, with a deadline he set."

"What deadline?"

"Friday."

Alexa looked at the bottle, and then at me. "Why Friday? If the deal is good for her, it is good for her next month."

"Now you are asking the right question. A man who is buying something fairly does not need the seller to decide by Friday. Deadlines exist in deals for one purpose: to keep the seller from doing what she did this morning, which is to walk into an office like this one and begin asking questions."

She wrote something on the pad, underneath the arithmetic, and did not show me what it was.

* *

She almost signed anyway.

I know because of the voicemail she left at 7:40 on Friday morning, in Spanish, at the speed of a woman who had not slept. I listened to it twice with my door closed, and when I came out for coffee, Alexa read my face before I said a word.

"María?"

"Osvaldo called her last night." I told her what I judged she needed to know, which was most of it, because the lesson in it belonged to her as much as to anyone. He had not been angry; that was the part that had frightened María. He had been warm, warmer than ever. He had raised the offer to fifty thousand dollars, moved the deadline to five o'clock that afternoon, and told her that after five o'clock he would have to explore other options for the category, which is a sentence he did not compose himself. She had sat at her kitchen table until two in the morning with the folder open and a pen in her hand, doing the same arithmetic Alexa had done on the legal pad, except that María's arithmetic had rent in it, and Camila's tuition, and eleven years of being tired. She said the pen touched the paper. She said she thought of her mother writing FORTALECEDOR on a piece of tape.

She did not sign. She had written the four pages instead. "*Las hice todas, Licenciado,*" she said on the recording. I did them all. She would bring them on Monday, and she wanted to know, please, what she should say to Osvaldo at five o'clock.

Alexa was quiet for a while, holding her coffee with both hands.

"He raised his own offer by twenty-five percent," she said finally. "In four days. Nobody countered. Nobody negotiated. She never even called him back." She looked past me, into my office, at the amber bottle still sitting where María had left it, unlabeled now, catching the morning light like the thing in a museum they build the alarms around. "On Tuesday, she apologized for it."

"Write that down," I said.

She already was.

CHAPTER TWO
Four Doors

On Monday morning, María Restrepo returned to my office with four handwritten pages and the report of a telephone call.

She had called Osvaldo at five minutes before five on Friday afternoon, because she did not want him to believe she was playing games with his deadline. She told him she was not saying no. She told him she was taking an inventory, that a lawyer was helping her understand what she owned, and that she would come back to him when she understood it. She had practiced the sentences in the car, she admitted, the way she had once practiced sentences for the citizenship interview.

"And what did he say?"

"He was nice." She said the word carefully, the way a person handles something with tongs. "He said, of course, take your time, family comes first. Then he said, 'You understand the fifty was for Friday.' When I finish my inventory, the offer is forty again." She folded her hands in her lap. "And then he asked me one more thing. He asked me the name of my lawyer."

"What did you tell him?"

"Your name." Worry crossed her face. "Was that wrong? He asked so politely."

"It was not wrong. It was information he wanted, and now he has it, and now we know that he wanted it." I wrote the question down, because polite questions are still questions, and a buyer who asks for the name of the seller's lawyer is measuring the ground the way a surveyor measures it, quietly, before anyone builds anything. "Señora, none of this should frighten you. Friday taught us two useful things. It taught us that the deadline was never real, because the man walked past his own deadline the moment it failed to work. And it taught us that the price moves. The price that rose once because you went quiet can rise again for better reasons. Now show me the pages."

They were written in Spanish, in a round and patient hand, on paper borrowed from Camila's school notebook. The first page told me that the difference lived in three places: an ingredient, a way of preparing it, and a waiting, by which she meant time that had to pass and could not be hurried. She had written the categories and nothing more, exactly as instructed, and at the bottom of the page she had drawn a small padlock, which no one had instructed.

The second page held names. María. Camila, most of it. Luz, the steps but not the amounts. Then came a fourth entry I had not expected, written smaller than the others: *el cuaderno de mamá*. Her mother's notebook. Marta had kept one after all, in the same blue ballpoint that labeled the bottles, and María had carried it to Miami after the funeral, in a suitcase with the photographs. It lived in a shoebox in her bedroom closet. Beneath that entry, in different ink and different handwriting, someone had added a line: *y las fotos en mi teléfono*. And the photos on my phone. Camila had photographed some of the pages two years earlier, to keep a copy safe, and the copy now lived wherever telephones keep the things we ask them to keep.

The third page was the sales history. I read the first line, and then I set the page aside, deliberately, the way you set aside an envelope when you already suspect what the result inside will say. That page would need its own meeting, and I told her so.

"Saturday morning," I said. "Your kitchen. You, Camila, one hour, and one piece of paper with four columns on it. I want to see where the product is made, and I want your daughter in the room when we sort what your family owns, because half of what we are sorting is her inheritance."

"You would come to the apartment?"

"Señora, for two weeks the asset has been coming to the lawyer. It is time the lawyer went to the asset."

* *

Alexa learned about Saturday from the calendar, because Saturday appeared on it as a house call, and house calls did not otherwise appear on it.

"Take me with you."

"No."

"I'll sit in the kitchen and say nothing. I'm basically furniture."

"You are an employee of a law firm, and it is a client's home and a client's business. The rule from last week did not expire over the weekend."

She leaned against the doorframe with her arms crossed, and I watched her decide not to argue the point she could not win. "Fine," she said. "Then teach me here. Whatever you're going to draw on her paper Saturday, draw it for me first. Not her facts. The system. If I'm going to answer your phones, I should at least know what the building sells."

That was fair, and I told her so, and I stood at the whiteboard in the small conference room and drew four doors.

"Everything this office does for a family like hers passes through one of four doors," I said. "The law gives an owner four different ways to hold an idea, and they are not interchangeable, and choosing the wrong one costs more than choosing none."

"Door one." I wrote the word PATENT. "The loudest door. A patent is a trade with the government. You teach the world, completely and in public, how to make and use your invention, and in exchange you receive roughly twenty years in which no one may make it, use it, or sell it without your permission. No one. Even a stranger who invents the same thing honestly, in his own garage, with no copying at all, is locked out. It is the strongest right American law offers an inventor, and the price is the teaching. When the twenty years end, the invention belongs to everyone, forever."

"Door two." I wrote TRADE SECRET. "The silent door. A trade secret is information that has value because it is not generally known, and that you guard with reasonable effort. There is no filing, no fee, no application, and no expiration. Guard it well and it can outlive everyone in this building. But the protection is conditional. It punishes only wrongful taking. If a competitor buys your product and figures out the formula on a laboratory bench, the law shakes his hand. If someone invents the same thing independently, the law congratulates him. And one careless disclosure can end the whole thing, permanently, because a secret that stops being secret does not come back."

"Door three." TRADEMARK. "The door most people underestimate, because it does not protect the product at all. It protects the name. A trademark tells customers where a thing comes from, and its strength runs on a spectrum. An invented word is strong. A word that merely describes the product is weak, and a generic word can never be owned by anyone. Here is what matters most: renew it and police it, and a trademark can last as long as the family does. A competitor who copies the chemistry can never legally sell it under your name, to the customers who trust your name. For a business built on trust, the name often ends up worth more than the recipe."

"Door four." COPYRIGHT. "The door people believe they have already walked through. Copyright protects original expression. Photographs, labels, videos, the story you write about your grandmother. It does not protect a method. It protects the way something is said, never the thing the words teach you to do."

Alexa studied the board the way she studies everything, looking for the seam. "My *abuela* has flan de coco on an index card," she said. "Her handwriting, her card. That card is copyrighted, right?"

"The card, more or less. The flan, not at all. Copyright would stop a stranger from photocopying the card and selling the copies. It would not stop him from reading the card, baking the flan, and selling the flan on the same street."

"That's the part nobody believes."

"That is the part that costs people the most. They write the recipe down, they feel protected, and they have confused the paper with the thing the paper describes."

She took a picture of the whiteboard with her phone. Then she asked the question I had been waiting for since I picked up the marker. "Okay. So, which one do we file first?"

"You have the order backward. First the map, then the vessel, then, and only then, the filing. People walk into law offices every day and pay good money to file the wrong thing, because filing feels like action and understanding feels like delay. A lawyer who takes that money without asking what actually fits is not on their side."

"You realize that's the least satisfying answer you could give me."

"It is also the least expensive one you will ever receive from a lawyer. Write it down anyway."

* *

The apartment smelled like a kitchen that worked for a living, steam and something green and something faintly sweet underneath, and I made a point of not asking what any of it was. Two induction burners stood where most kitchens kept a toaster. Amber bottles waited in plastic crates by the door, four crates high. On the refrigerator, held by a magnet from a Medellín bakery, hung a photograph of a woman with María's eyes and a stricter mouth. Marta. The blue ballpoint had come from somewhere, and it had come from her.

Camila answered the door in a hoodie from a college whose tuition I now understood to be part of every calculation in this family. She was twenty-four, she studied accounting at night, and she shook my hand like a person who has read articles about shaking hands. Within five minutes I understood the division of labor in the household: María owned the pots, and Camila owned everything with a screen.

María wanted to show me the preparation. She had the first pot ready, and she reached for a canister with genuine hospitality, and I stopped her with a raised hand.

"The fewer heads that hold it, the stronger it is," I said. "That includes this head. I am your lawyer. I do not need to be your confidant."

We sat at the kitchen table, and Camila tore a sheet from an easel pad left over from a school project, and across the top I wrote four words: PATENT. TRADE SECRET. TRADEMARK. COPYRIGHT. Then we began to sort the family's possessions, the ones that had never appeared on any tax return.

Camila went first, and she went straight at it. "We always said we'd patent it. That was the plan since I was little. Abuela's formula, patented, like on the commercials. Why isn't everything in column one?"

So, I gave her the trade I had given Alexa, the twenty loud years and the price of the teaching, and then I told them about the two guards who stood at that door. "The first guard asks whether the invention is genuinely new, because nature and old knowledge belong to everyone. The second guard asks a harder question. He asks what you have already done. An invention that has already been commercialized, sold, put on the market, is generally no longer new in the eyes of the law, and the door closes, and it does not reopen." I let that sit for a moment. "Your family has been selling this formula for nine years in this country, and your grandmother sold it in Medellín for decades before that. On Monday, your mother and I will walk through that history carefully, sale by sale, because the details matter and I do not guess about doors. But I will not let you decorate a locked door either. For the original formula, the honest expectation is that the patent door closed years ago, quietly, while everyone was busy working."

Camila sat back. "So, we lost it. Before we even knew it existed, we lost it."

"You lost one door out of four, probably, and here is what should interest an accounting student. The same history that locks the patent door barely matters to the door beside it. The secret door does not ask whether you sold the product. It asks only whether the formula itself stayed unknown, and it has. Nine years of sales closed one door and left the other standing open. And keep one more thing in your pocket for later: if this family ever creates a new version, a genuine improvement that has never been sold to anyone, that improvement arrives at the patent door with a clean history. The original formula's past does not follow it."

María, who had been quiet, asked the practical question. "Then the formula goes in column two."

"The formula, the process, the waiting, and one thing your first page taught me." I looked at her. "The source. Where the ingredient comes from, and from whom. A competitor with the recipe but the wrong source has the words to the song and not the voice. Suppliers go in column two."

We moved to the third column, and it was the third column that changed the temperature of the room.

"What is the product's name?" I asked.

Mother and daughter looked at each other. "It doesn't have one," Camila said. "The tape says FORTALECEDOR, but that's just, like, the word. The salons call it *el de Doña María.* Everybody just says that. The one from Doña María."

"Then listen to what you just told me. Your customers built you a brand and have been saying it out loud for nine years, and no one in this family has ever tried to own it. FORTALECEDOR itself is a warning, not a name. A word that merely describes what a product does is the weakest kind of mark there is, and Spanish words and family names carry their own trapdoors at the trademark office, which will get an afternoon of its own. But before we leave this column, I want you both to notice something about Osvaldo's paper." I did not need the folder to quote it. "Paragraph seven did not ask for the recipe. Paragraph seven asked for the names María and Doña María, your face, and your family's story, forever and worldwide. The only man who has ever appraised this business told you, in writing, which asset he valued. Read his offer as a map of what to protect."

Camila pulled the easel sheet toward her and wrote *Doña María* in the third column, and underneath it she wrote a question mark, and I watched her circle the question mark twice. "I want this one," she said. "The name. Finding the real one. I have opinions."

"You will need more than opinions, but yes. That project is yours, and it starts after Monday."

The fourth column took the shortest time and left the longest silence. Into it went the future label, the photographs, the story of Marta that someone would someday write for the back of a box. And into it, with an asterisk, went the notebook.

"The notebook is two things at once," I said. "As pages, as your grandmother's handwriting and words, it is expression, and expression is what copyright protects. No one can photocopy those pages and sell them. But the method the pages describe receives nothing from that column. A stranger who reads the notebook may make everything in it, legally, forever. Which means the notebook's real importance is not in column four at all. It is a written copy of column two. It is the secret, on paper, in a shoebox."

Camila had gone still. María noticed it before I did.

"*Las fotos*," María said quietly.

"The photos," Camila said. "I photographed some pages after Abuela died. I was scared of losing it. They're in my phone, which means they're in my backup, which means they're in the cloud, which means I don't actually know where they are." She looked at me. "How bad is that?"

"It is not a fire. It is a window someone left open, and we will spend a whole session on windows soon enough. Today we do two things that cost nothing. First, the spreading stops now. No new copies, no sharing, and the notebook comes out of the shoebox. Bring it to my office on Monday and we will decide where it should live. Second, you both remember this feeling, because a secret is not a possession, it is a practice, and today is the day the practice started."

María looked at her daughter, and something passed between them in Spanish without a word of Spanish being spoken, and then the doorbell rang.

* *

It was her cousin Reina, who lived two buildings over, and with Reina came a young man in very white sneakers carrying his phone in a small tripod, the way other men carry keys.

I turned our easel sheet face down on the table, and the meeting became coffee.

His name was Victor. He was a friend of Reina's son, he was twenty-six, and two hundred thousand people watched him on the internet, a number he delivered within the first ninety seconds, the way other men mention where they went to school. He made hair videos. Transformations, routines, product reviews, and lately, he said something bigger, because in three weeks he was launching his own line.

"Formulated by me," he said, accepting coffee. "No middlemen, no gatekeepers. I found a factory online, bro, amazing price, five thousand units minimum, and they move fast. People wait years to launch. I don't wait."

María asked, politely, whether he had a lawyer helping him.

Victor smiled, the way people smile at their grandmother's superstitions. "Lawyers are brakes, señora. Respect, but that whole world is for after you're big. Right now, speed is the moat. Content is the moat. I put out three videos a week. By the time anybody copies me, I'm three products ahead. You can't paperwork your way to that. You have to *move*."

I asked him how he had chosen the factory.

"Price. And the vibes were good."

I asked him what the factory had agreed to keep confidential.

"They're cool. We have a group chat." He turned the tripod toward himself briefly, checked something on the screen, and turned it back. "Look, I get it. Papers, columns, whatever this is." He nodded at the upside-down easel sheet with a generosity that cost him nothing. "But I filmed myself mixing the formula last month. Full video. People love process content. That video did more for my brand than any lawyer ever did for anybody."

"Who owns the formula you mixed on camera?" I asked.

"Me. Obviously. It's my channel."

He said it with total confidence, and I let it stand, because there is a kind of certainty that cannot hear anything while it is performing, and the kindest thing you can do is not make it perform harder. He invited us all to the launch. He was gone in twenty minutes, with Reina, in a small weather system of cologne.

The kitchen was quiet. María turned the easel sheet face up again and looked at the four columns for a long time, at the padlock her own hand had drawn, at *Doña María* with the circle around the question mark.

"Victor has two hundred thousand people," she said, "and no columns. I have four columns and no name."

"You have four columns, a name the customers already say, and a buyer whose own contract told you what to protect," I said. "On Monday we find out what the past has already decided. After that, we build."

* *

On Sunday night, Victor posted the video announcing his launch, and by Monday morning Alexa had watched it twice, because I had mentioned no names and no facts, and she had found him anyway, the way her generation finds anything, in about four minutes, from the word *hair* and the word *launch.*

"Four hundred thousand views," she said, setting my coffee down next to the amber bottle, which had not moved from the corner of my desk. "He holds the bottles up to the camera. You can read every label. He gives the amounts. He does the steps in order, and then he says, quote, this is my secret formula." She straightened up. "Three generations kept theirs in their heads. He put his in the description box."

"And he is certain it belongs to him," I said, "which is a different question, and one that will find him before he goes looking for it."

Alexa glanced at the clock because she had learned the calendar by then. María was due at nine, with her mother's notebook in her purse and nine years of history to walk through, sale by sale, and somewhere across town a distributor who knew my name was waiting to learn what his forty thousand dollars had failed to buy.

CHAPTER THREE
What the Past Already Cost

María Restrepo arrived at nine o'clock on Monday with her mother's notebook wrapped in a dish towel, and with her daughter, who arrived with a laptop and forty names.

"For the brand," Camila said, setting the laptop on my conference table before anyone sat down. "I made a list. I ranked them. There's a spreadsheet."

"There will be a whole meeting for the spreadsheet," I said. "Today we read the past. The naming starts the moment the audit ends, and not one minute before, because I am not going to let this family build a beautiful door on a foundation we have not inspected."

Camila closed the laptop with the expression of a person filing an objection for the record. María, meanwhile, had unwrapped the dish towel, and the room went quiet on its own.

The notebook was small and swollen, the way notebooks become when they have lived in kitchens. Its cover had once been red. She opened it only far enough to show me the first page, and I saw the blue ballpoint I already knew from a strip of masking tape, the same careful capitals, and I held up my hand before the page could turn any further.

"That is enough. I did not read past the cover, and for the same reason I did not watch the pots on Saturday." I brought out the pad I had prepared. "Here is what happens to it. This week, you rent a safe-deposit box at your bank, in your name, and the notebook lives there. Not in a shoebox, not in this office, not in anyone's purse. We keep a simple record of every copy that exists in the world, which at the moment means the notebook, and some photographs on a telephone, and nothing else, and it stays that way. A secret is not a possession. It is a practice."

"Camila already deleted the photos," María said, with a mother's speed.

"Camila deleted what she could see," Camila corrected, and looked at me. "I killed the backup too, but I'm not going to sit here and swear to a lawyer that a copy doesn't exist somewhere in a server farm in Oregon. I can't know that. Nobody can."

"Which is the correct answer," I said, "and the last honest inventory this family took was four pages long, so let us keep the streak alive. Señora, take out the third page."

* *

The third page was the sales history, and we walked it backward, sale by sale, the way I had promised.

It began nine years ago with a folding table at her church, after a Sunday service, eleven bottles at ten dollars each, because a woman from the choir had insisted. It grew through the cousins, then through the neighborhood, then through the two salons, whose owners started with six bottles on consignment and now ordered by the case. Four years ago came Osvaldo, who found the product in one of those salons and asked the owner where it came from. Two years of wholesale followed, invoiced at twelve dollars, paid on time. Somewhere in the middle were the two seasons at the street festival, cash in a cigar box, and the sister in Queens, who began by buying six bottles a month for herself and her neighbors and now, María admitted, bought thirty and sold them at eighteen.

"Eighteen," Camila said, writing it down. "She charges eighteen and we charge fourteen. In New York. For nine years, Mamá."

"She has expenses," María said.

I asked the next question carefully, because I already knew it was the one she had dressed up. "Señora, the church sales. Tell me about those again."

Her hands found the hem of her blouse. "Those were not really sales," she said. "It was among friends. They gave me something for the bottles. Contributions. It was not a business, it was..." She looked for a word that would make it smaller. "It was community."

"Did the bottles change hands, and did money come back?"

"Yes, but."

"Then the law calls it a sale, señora, no matter what the choir calls it, and I need you to hear why I will not let you soften it. Everything we build from today stands on this page. If we prettify history now, we are not protecting you, we are hiding a crack in your own foundation from your own engineer. The tax questions, if there are any, are a separate conversation for another day, and they are survivable. What is not survivable is a lawyer who plans around a past his client curated for him." I let the silence do its work. "So. Is there anything else on this page wearing a costume?"

María was quiet for a long moment. Then she said, "The festival was three seasons, not two. The first year was small. I did not count it because it embarrassed me."

"Thank you. Now the page is true."

And then I told them what the true page meant, because they had earned the verdict in full.

"On Saturday I told you the patent door had probably closed. Today we can retire the word probably. The rule is simple and it is merciless. An invention that has been on sale loses its newness, and in this country an inventor gets, at most, a single year of grace after her own first sale to file. One year. Your first sale was nine years ago at a folding table, and your mother was selling the same formula in Medellín when you were a girl. The law does not care that the sales were small, or friendly, or cash, or that the buyers were from the choir. It does not even care if the sale was quiet and the buyer promised to keep it confidential. A sale is a sale. For the original formula, the patent door is closed, it closed years ago, and no lawyer, including this one, can reopen it. Anyone who takes your money promising otherwise is not selling you law. He is selling you hope with a filing fee."

Camila had stopped typing. María, to my surprise, had not flinched at all. She sat with her hands folded, and when she finally spoke, she nodded toward the notebook on the table.

"My mother never wanted it in an office," she said. "She used to say, *lo que es de la casa, se queda en la casa.*" What belongs to the house stays in the house. "You are telling me the law agrees with her."

"I am telling you the door she would have chosen is the one still open, and that her granddaughter should now hear the other half, because the other half is the reason nobody cries at this table today." I turned the sales page around, so it faced them. "Camila. You are studying accounting. Forget the law for five minutes and read this page as numbers."

She pulled it toward her, and I watched the accounting student wake up inside the mourner. "Nine years of revenue with zero advertising spend," she said slowly. "Repeat customers. A wholesale account that found us. A reseller in another state marking us up almost thirty percent and still moving inventory. Price stuck at fourteen dollars since, apparently, forever, which means demand at fourteen is proven and demand above fourteen has literally never been tested." She looked up. "This isn't a confession. It's a market study."

"It is the market study money cannot buy, because no one can fake nine years of strangers coming back. Last week a man on the internet showed four hundred thousand people a formula and called the views proof. Views are enthusiasm. This page is validation, and the difference between those two words is going to be a whole afternoon of your lives very soon." I took the page back. "One more thing before you go to the bank. Señora, has Osvaldo said anything since Friday?"

"He placed his usual order," María said. "Two cases, like always. As if nothing happened."

"As if nothing happened," I repeated, and wrote it down. "A man who needed you to decide by Friday is still buying by the case on Monday. Remember that the next time his paper tries to hurry you."

* *

Carlos came on Wednesday, sent by a barber in Doral who had told him that I helped people like him. He was fifty-eight years old, from Valencia, Venezuela, and he carried his entire past in a clear plastic sleeve: two faded labels, a photograph of a small production floor with everything squared to everything else, and a price list from 2009 in a currency that no longer meant anything.

He addressed me as doctor, in the Venezuelan way, and he sat like a man at an interview he had rehearsed for six years.

"I will not waste your time, Doctor. In Valencia I invented a hair treatment. A restorative cream. Eighteen years. I sold it in pharmacies and barbershops in Carabobo, Aragua, part of Lara. People did not ask for a cream, they asked for *el Uzcátegui.* My surname. That was the brand, because I never needed another one." He aligned the plastic sleeve with the edge of my desk. "I controlled everything. I designed the mixing equipment myself. I measured everything. When the situation in my country ate the business, I closed it correctly, I paid what I owed, and I came here. For six years I have driven a delivery truck, I have saved, and I have told no one the formula. Not my wife. I mixed alone, always, at night, with the door locked. Because my plan was to do it correctly this time." He looked at me with the pride of a man arriving at the summit of a very long climb. "First the patent. Then the launch. In that order. Correctly."

There is a particular silence that comes before you take something from a careful man, and I have never learned a way around it, only through it.

"Don Carlos," I said, "before anything else, I want you to know that what I am about to tell you is not a verdict on you. It is a verdict on a door. The patent law of this country asks whether an invention is new, and eighteen years of sales answer that question, and the answer does not improve because the sales happened in Carabobo instead of Florida. The rule reaches sales anywhere in the world. Your formula was on the market for eighteen years. For the original formula, the American patent door is closed, and it was closed before you ever boarded the plane."

He did not move for a moment. Then he did something worse than arguing. He nodded, once, the way men nod when a suspicion they have carried quietly is finally confirmed, and he began to slide his labels back into the plastic sleeve.

"Then I have wasted your time after all, Doctor. And six years of my own." He stood. "In Valencia I had three states asking for my name. I had the equipment. I had pharmacies. If I had come here earlier, or filed earlier, or known earlier." He stopped himself, because the list had no bottom. "Millions, Doctor. I left millions on a table in a country that no longer exists, and now you tell me the table followed me here. Better I keep driving the truck. At least the truck does not pretend."

"Sit down for one more minute," I said. "You came for a patent, and the patent is gone, so now let me tell you what you actually own, because you are a careful man and your inventory is wrong."

He remained standing, but he did not leave.

"First. Who knows the formula?"

"No one. I told you. I mixed alone."

"Then understand what you just said. For eighteen years of production and six years of waiting, through employees and pharmacies and a national collapse and emigration, the formula never left your head. The same caution you are cursing right now is the reason your most valuable asset survived the trip. The door your history closed is the loud one. The silent door does not ask whether you sold the product. It asks whether the formula stayed unknown, and you, Don Carlos, are possibly the most qualified secret-keeper who has ever walked into this office. Second. Your brand. People in three states asked for *el Uzcátegui*. Tell me, when you drive your truck through Doral, what do you hear on the sidewalks?"

He looked at me. "Spanish. My Spanish."

"Your customers emigrated with you. The pharmacist from Valencia is here. The barber who sent you to me is here. The men who asked for your name by name are ten minutes from this office, buying inferior products from strangers, because the man they trusted believes his past disqualified him. Your history did not only close a door. It proved, for eighteen years, in three states, that people pay for what you make.

Nobody launching from zero has that, and everybody launching from zero would trade for it. And third, so that you leave here with the whole map: the old formula cannot be patented, but you have not stopped thinking in six years, and I suspect a man who designs his own equipment has improvements in a drawer. A genuine improvement that has never been sold arrives at the patent door with a clean history. Your past does not follow it through."

Carlos looked at the plastic sleeve in his hands for a long time. When he sat back down, he sat slowly, the way a man lowers something heavy that he has decided not to throw away after all.

"The equipment," he said. "The new mixing method. I redesigned it in my head on the night shifts. It does not exist anywhere. I have never built it, never sold it, never spoken of it." He looked up. "That one is clean, Doctor?"

"That one," I said, "we walk through properly, in order, and this time the order will be correct from the first day. But not this week. This week you go home and you write me the same four pages a woman from Medellín wrote me last week, and you do not put the formula on any of them."

For the first time he had entered, something that was not grief crossed his face. "There are others," he said. "Like me."

"Don Carlos," I said, "you have no idea."

* *

Alexa was at the front desk when he left, and she waited a full ten minutes before appearing in my doorway, which for her was an act of monumental restraint.

"The gentleman with the plastic sleeve came in looking like a funeral and left looking like a Tuesday," she said. "I'm not asking what was said. I'm asking what the pattern is, because that's twice this week the building did that to somebody."

So, I taught her the pattern, in the only form I could and the only form she needed, with no names attached. "Two kinds of people find this office," I said. "People with history and no audience, and people with an audience and no history. The second kind believes attention is proof. The first kind believes their past is a debt. Both are wrong in opposite directions. A real sales history is the most valuable document a small business owns, even when, especially when, it closes a legal door, because it answers the only question that kills most companies. Not can we make it. Who will pay for it, at what price, again."

"Speaking of the second kind." She held up her phone. "Victor posted his pre-order page last night. Guess the number of units."

"Five thousand."

"Five thousand. The exact minimum the factory made him buy. His validation is his invoice." She lowered the phone. "He's got two hundred thousand people watching and no idea if a single one of them will pay fourteen dollars for anything. Meanwhile the lady with the amber bottle has nine years of people paying and doesn't have two hundred followers." Alexa looked at the bottle in the corner of my desk. "Somebody should introduce those two problems to each other."

"Somebody is about to," I said. "Saturday, we find out exactly who has been buying that bottle for nine years, and why, and what they would say if the price were not fourteen dollars. Before this family spends its first real dollar, we are going to know the customer's name."

She wrote that down. Then she did not leave, which is how I knew the meeting was not over.

"Two kinds," she said. "You said two. I want to ask about a third one, and I want to say in advance that I found this in the mail, which is my job, and that I read the outside of the envelope, which is also my job, and then I read the inside, which possibly was not."

She put a single sheet of paper on my desk. It was a renewal notice from a marketing company, and it was addressed to me.

I looked at it for what I am told was a while.

"Ask," I said.

"The señora sold bottles for nine years and apologized for it. The truck driver kept a secret for twenty-four years and called it a waste." Alexa tapped the page once. "This says you've been paying somebody two thousand eight hundred dollars a month since I was in high school, plus whatever the second number is. And the last three lines are a renewal that already happened."

* *

I want to set this down carefully, because I have asked two people this week to give me a true page, and it would be a poor sort of lawyer who kept his own.

But I have to start earlier than the marketing company, because the marketing company does not make sense on its own.

Thirteen years ago another vehicle came through an intersection and found mine, and I spent a season being repaired. I recovered, and I am not going to make it larger than it was. But there were weeks in there that I remember the way you remember a room you walked through in the dark, and somewhere inside those weeks I decided that what I needed was a car.

Not transportation. I had transportation. What I wanted was a vehicle worthy of a crash. I have never found a better description of a man deciding something from inside an injury, so I will leave the phrase where it is. I did not shop for where it could take me. I shopped for what it could survive. The company that sold it attached a promise to the purchase: that I would fly to another country and collect the thing myself, at the factory, which is exactly the sort of detail that turns a deposit into an appointment instead of a payment. I sent the money while I was still medicated. I never made the trip. I never took delivery. To this day I have not laid eyes on the vehicle I bought.

I am not going to tell you what the deposit was, because the number would let you off. Here is the part that mattered. I learned that I have a self who signs things. He does not appear on a calendar. He shows up when I am hurt, or hurried, or flattered, and he is confident, and he is efficient, and he had been living in me the whole time and I had never been introduced. That is what happens to a man who believes his life has no chapter nine. That there is no later. That nothing gets billed.

Seven years ago, he came back to work.

* *

A man came to this office with a proposal, and I want to be fair to him about how he did it, because the fairness is the mechanism.

He did not oversee it. There was no chart of what my competitors were spending, no promise of clients, no adjectives. He was spare and calm and slightly bored, and a man who does not need to persuade you reads as a man who does not need to. That is the whole trick, and it is better than enthusiasm, and it worked on a person who has spent his career watching people be persuaded.

The agreement was thirty-six months. A monthly retainer of twenty-eight hundred dollars. Advertising money billed through his company on top of the retainer.

I read the fee schedule.

I want you to notice that sentence, because it is the entire confession. I read the fee schedule the way María read Osvaldo's four pages: I found the number, I decided the number was survivable, and I let a quiet man explain the rest of it to me out loud.

There was exactly one figure in that whole arrangement that I understood completely, and it was the one I paid. The advertising spend. I could tell you to the dollar what went out the door every month, because that number spoke a language I had been fluent in since law school. Money leaving.

Everything that came back was in another language.

Impressions. Reach. Click-through rate. Cost per thousand. Quality score. Bounce rate. Attribution window. Every month a report arrived containing those words and true numbers beside them, and I read it the way you read a wine list in a country whose alphabet you do not have. The numbers went up. When they went down, there was a reason, and the reason also used the words.

I was never lied to. I want to be precise about that, because it is the most useful thing in this chapter. Nobody put a false figure in front of me in three years. I was being reported to in a vocabulary where lying is unnecessary, because none of the words could be checked against anything that happens in an office. Impressions are real. They are also not a client. There are no number of impressions that becomes a signed matter, and there is no month in which impressions go down because nobody called.

And I never asked. That is the sentence I would delete if I were kind to myself. A lawyer earns his living by asking the question that makes him look stupid, in front of judges, in front of clients, in front of opposing counsel who would love nothing more. I stopped asking it here. Not because he discouraged me; he did not. Because it was my money and my firm and my name on the door, and there is a particular silence a man keeps when the question he needs to ask would require him to admit that he has been buying something for eleven months without knowing what it is.

That silence cost more than the retainer.

* *

Then there is the part I could have known for free, which is the part that was written down.

There was no performance obligation. The agreement promised *services*, and services were not defined anywhere in the document in any way a person could measure, which meant the company could satisfy that contract completely without producing one client, and did.

The advertising money passed through at a management percentage. Read that twice, the way I did not. The more of my money they spent, the more they earned. I had signed a document that paid a man a commission on my own losses.

The term renewed automatically for twelve months unless I gave written notice ninety days before the end. I did not calendar that date, because I did not know the date existed, because I had not read the paragraph it lived in. I found out about the renewal in an envelope, in month thirty-seven, which is the same way my niece found out about it seven years later.

And the accounts were in their name. All of them. The advertising account, the tracking number, the landing pages, the analytics history.

Years of information about who was looking for a lawyer in this county and what words they used to look, and when I finally ended it, I walked away with nothing. Not a spreadsheet. Not a phone number. I had not sold that history. I had never owned it. I had paid, monthly, to build an asset inside somebody else's house.

There is an old joke about a man who gets sold the London Bridge. The joke is too generous. The London Bridge at least exists, and you can stand on it.

The total, over three years and one month, was fifty-one thousand and change.

I have memorized the number. That is not a good sign about a number.

* *

The money is the smaller loss, and I want to be honest about that too, because the money is the part that sounds like a story and the rest is the part that actually happened.

While I was buying impressions, two firms within a mile of this office were doing the slow thing. One started answering questions on video, badly at first, in the language the sidewalk actually speaks. The other started a list and wrote to it every month and kept writing when nothing happened, which is the part nobody photographs. Neither of them was smarter than me. They were simply somewhere else with those three years.

You cannot audit that loss. It never arrives as a line item. There is no invoice that reads *the people who would have found you in those thirty-seven months and found someone else instead*, and there is no motion I can file to bring them back. They are somebody's clients now. They are happy. They should be.

The señora's first sale closed a patent door nine years before she knew there was a door. Don Carlos's closed in Valencia while he was doing everything else correctly. Mine closed in a conference room, on a Tuesday, while I was nodding.

And on Monday of this week, at that table, I told a young woman studying accounting that views are enthusiasm and a sales page is validation, and I said it the way a man says something he read in a book.

I did not read it in a book. It cost fifty-one thousand dollars and three years, and I paid for it in impressions.

* *

Alexa was still in the doorway when I finished, holding her notebook and not writing in it, which for her is a flag at half-mast.

"So, which one are you?" she said. "Because I've been keeping the list of the two kinds, and I don't have a column for a guy who reads contracts for a living."

"Neither. I am the third kind, and the third kind is worse, because the third kind cannot even claim he did not know how. I did not lack the skill. I lacked ten minutes and one question." I put the notice in the file where it belongs, which is the file I keep for things I do not intend to forget. "So here is the rule that came out of it, and you will hear it in this building until you hate the sound of it. Never accept a report in a language you cannot audit. If a number cannot go down for a reason you understand, it is not a measurement. It is a decoration."

"And the car?" she said. Because she is my sister's daughter, and she does not leave the loose thread alone.

"The car taught me that there is a version of me who signs things. The contract taught me that he does not need me to be injured. He will do it stone sober on a Tuesday afternoon, in a good suit, in my own conference room, if nobody in the room is willing to say *I don't know what that word means.*" I capped the pen. "Your job at that desk is not answering the phone. Your job is to be the person in the room who says it."

She wrote that down. Then she paused at the door.

"The truck driver," she said. "Not his file, not his facts, I know. Just tell me one thing. Did he quit?"

"He almost did," I said. "Then he counted what was left."

"And you?"

"I am still counting," I said. "Go home, Alexa."

PART II

THE OPPORTUNITY

CHAPTER FOUR
The Market Is a Person

On Friday afternoon I gave my niece an assignment, and for the first time all summer she did not look at me the way jurors look at a weak witness.

"I want twenty questions," I told her. "A kit. The questions a small business should ask the customers it already has, before it spends its first real dollar chasing customers it does not. No client, no facts, no names. Build the instrument and build it so that a person who has never done research in her life could pick it up and use it on a Tuesday."

"Why me?"

"Because you found a stranger's video channel in four minutes from two words, and because you keep telling me information is free. Prove it. Show me what the free tools can actually do in the hands of somebody who knows where they are."

She came back Monday with eleven questions, not twenty, and a page of handwriting that had been crossed out and rewritten so many times it looked like a treaty.

"Twenty was the wrong number," she said, dropping into the chair across from my desk. "I tested it this weekend on Abuela. About her flan. Controlled experiment, no stakes, and it fell apart in four minutes. I asked her why people love her flan and I got the history of the parish since 1987. Opinions are useless, Profe. Everybody's an expert on their own opinions. So, I threw out every question that starts with why do you think and rewrote them to start with tell me about the last time. The last time you bought it. The last time you ran out. What you said, word for word, when you told your sister about it. People lie about their opinions without knowing they're lying. They can't lie about last Tuesday."

I read the eleven questions. They were good. Two of them were better than good, and one of them was going to matter more than she knew.

"Number nine," I said. "Read it to me."

"What do you believe it does?" She shrugged. "That one's for marketing. Whatever they say, that's your ad copy. Free, from the mouths of the customers."

"That one," I said, "is for marketing and for me, and when the answers come back, you will understand why a lawyer wanted it on the list. Print it clean. It goes to work tomorrow."

* *

The argument on Saturday began before the coffee did.

María and Camila arrived at the office at nine, and I put a single sheet of paper in the middle of the conference table and asked the only question on the agenda. "Before this family spends one dollar on bottles, labels, or lawyers, I want a name and a face. Who is the customer?"

"Everyone," María said, comfortably. "Everyone has hair, and everyone's hair suffers in this country. The water here, the air conditioning. The product is for everybody."

"Nobody is for everybody," Camila said. "Mamá, that's not a market, that's a census." She opened the laptop. "The customer is twenty-two to thirty-four, female, on her phone three hours a day, buys from videos. That's where the growth is. That's who Victor has. If we're not talking to her, we're building a museum."

"Victor has an audience," I said. "You have buyers. Those are different species, and only one of them has ever given your family money. So here is what we are not going to do. We are not going to guess at this table. The two of you hold something almost no launching business on earth holds, which is nine years of living customers, and this week you are going to go ask them who they are." I slid the sheet across. Eleven questions printed clean. "Not opinions. Stories. The last time they bought, the last time they ran out, what they said, word for word, when they recommended it. Fifteen interviews. The salons, the church, and, by telephone, three of the Queens' customers through your sister. Camila conducts, María opens doors and says nothing, because the moment the maker is in the room, people say what is kind instead of what is true."

"I say nothing?" María asked.

"You smile, you introduce, and you suffer in silence, señora. It is for one week. And Camila, one instruction on question nine. Whatever they tell you the product does, write it down exactly, in their words, even if it sounds impossible, even if it sounds like a miracle. Especially then."

Camila studied the sheet with the expression she used on the easel pad, hunting the seam. "These aren't marketing questions," she said slowly. "These are depositions."

"Everything is a deposition," I said, "if you listen carefully enough."

* *

They came back the following Saturday with seventeen interviews instead of fifteen, because two women at the church had refused to be left out, and Camila stood at the head of my conference table with the laptop open and the particular energy of a person whose homework has surprised her.

"Okay. First, the bad news, and the bad news is about me." She pulled up a chart. "The customer is not twenty-two and she is not on TikTok. I interviewed seventeen buyers. The youngest is thirty-nine. The center of the market is a woman between forty-five and sixty. She was born in Colombia or Venezuela or Ecuador, she has been in this country twenty or thirty years, and here is the part I didn't see coming. She isn't buying for herself. I mean, she is, but she's buying for three people. Herself, her mother, and a daughter or a sister or a niece, and in four cases out of seventeen she ships bottles to another state or another country. The purchase is her, but the household is three generations." Camila looked up. "I built her a profile. I call her Marisol. Forty-six. Found the product through a friend at church or her stylist, which means she has never once found it through an ad, because there have never been any ads. She distrusts pharmacy brands. She pays cash. She uses the word natural eleven times per conversation. And when she recommends it, she doesn't describe the product. She tells the story of her own hair, before and after, every single time. Seventeen out of seventeen. The product is the proof, but the story is the pitch."

"And what does Marisol call it?" I asked, although I knew.

"Nobody said FORTALECEDOR. Not one person. Fourteen out of seventeen said *el de Doña María.*" Camila let that sit. "The brand already exists, Profe was right, it's just never been written down. Which brings me to money, and Mamá, you're not going to like money." She changed the chart. "I did the thing the questions said to do. I asked five of them, before telling them the price, what they believed a bottle cost. Guesses: twenty, twenty-two, twenty-five, eighteen, and one said thirty because her niece pays thirty for something worse at the mall. Nobody guessed fourteen. We are the only people in this market who think this is a fourteen-dollar product."

"That question gets its own afternoon," I said, "and it will be one of the most uncomfortable afternoons of this entire project, so let it wait. Question nine. What do they believe it does?"

Camila's face did the thing I had been waiting for a week for. She scrolled to a page of quotations and turned the laptop toward me, proud as a prosecutor with a signed confession.

"This is the gold mine. Listen. Doña Carmen, sixty-one: it regrew my hair after the chemotherapy. Word for word, Profe, she cried when she said it. Señora Pacheco: it cured my daughter's dandruff when nothing from the pharmacy could. Three separate women: it repairs the damage from the keratin treatments. Repairs, cures, regrows. That's the campaign. We don't have to invent a single claim, the customers already wrote the advertising, we just print what they—"

"Stop," I said, gently, because there was no way to say it that would not take something from her, and I had taken enough from people at that table already. "Camila. What you found is real, and it matters, and I want every word preserved exactly as those women spoke it. And now I have to tell you about the hardest sentence in this entire project. The most powerful sentences your research found are sentences this family cannot print."

The room went still.

"There is a line in American law that divides everything sold in a bottle into two kingdoms. On one side are cosmetics, products that cleanse and beautify and change how the body looks. On the other side are drugs, products intended to treat disease or to change how the body works. The words on your label and in your ads are what decide which kingdom you live in, and the two kingdoms have entirely different laws, different costs, and different police. Regrows hair is a claim about changing how the body works. Cures dandruff is a claim about treating a condition. The moment those words come from the seller, the product stops being a cosmetic in the law's eyes, no matter what is actually in the bottle, and a family kitchen in Miami is not equipped to live in the drug kingdom. Repairs are interesting ones. Sometimes it can be said, depending on exactly what is meant and exactly how it is phrased, and the difference is narrow enough that it gets its own meeting."

"But it's true," Camila said. "Doña Carmen's hair. I saw the photos. She's not lying."

"Nobody said she was lying. Doña Carmen may say anything she likes, to anyone she likes, forever. She is a customer telling her story. The law watches the seller, not the choir. And before either of you feels cheated, look at what your seventeen interviews actually gave you. A customer with a name and a face. The price the market set was higher than you did. A brand fourteen people recited without being asked. And a fence line, drawn in advance, showing exactly where the ground stops being yours, before you print ten thousand labels on the wrong side of it. Victor is going to pay for this same map. You got it from seventeen conversations and a sheet of paper."

María, who had been silent the entire presentation, spoke for the first time. "Marisol," she said, trying the name. "Forty-six. Buys for her mother and her daughter." She smiled, slowly, at her own daughter. "*Mija*, you drove all over Miami for a week to discover me."

"Yeah," Camila said. "Believe me, I noticed."

* *

The last argument of the day was the one I had been saving, and it started with a question I already knew the answer to.

"Señora, is the strengthener the only product you make?"

María and Camila exchanged a look with an entire negotiation inside it. "There is also *la crema para las puntas*," María admitted. "For the ends. I make it for maybe ten customers, special ones. And a rinse, for after. Small batches."

"Three products," Camila said, leaning in. "That's a line, Profe. That's a brand family. We launch all three, we triple the shelf presence, my forty names have options for the whole—"

"How many bottles of the strengthener can your mother make in a month, correctly, at the quality that built nine years of customers, without help?"

Camila stopped. She knew the number, because she had built the spreadsheet. "Two hundred. Maybe two-twenty if December doesn't have a hurricane."

"And every hour spent on the cream and the rinse comes out of those two hundred. Every dollar of ingredients, every crate, every label you design, every question a customer asks. Here is the choice in front of this family, and it is a real choice, and I will draft the papers for whichever one you make. Launch three products to everyone, thin, or launch one product to Marisol, deep. The strengthener, the hero, the one with nine years of proof and seventeen witnesses, done so well and told so clearly that Marisol's sister in Barranquilla hears about it. The cream and the rinse do not die. They wait, as chapter two and chapter three, for a company strong enough to carry them."

It was María who answered, and she answered as the maker. "One," she said. "The one my mother made. When it can stand by itself, then its brothers can come." She looked at Camila. "*¿Estás de acuerdo?*"

Camila closed the laptop, which was how she signed things. "One hero," she said. "But I'm keeping the forty names. And for the record, Edgar's going to be unbearable about the crates. He already thinks he's the vice president of shipping."

"Who is Edgar?" I asked.

"My cousin," María said, warmly, gathering her purse. "Reina's brother. He has helped with everything since the beginning. He drives the deliveries, he built my table for the church, he carries the crates. He always says, when this becomes big, we did it together." She said it with love, and she said it on her way out the door, and so she did not see her lawyer stop writing.

I put a small mark next to Edgar's name. Some sentences are gifts, and some sentences are invoices that have not arrived yet, and after twenty years I can usually hear the difference.

* *

Victor launched that same week, on a Thursday, live, to everyone.

Alexa watched it happen in real time from the front desk, on her own phone, on her own break, and gave me the summary I had not asked for at the end of the day.

"Five products at once. The Fuego line. Shampoo, conditioner, a mask, an oil, and the hero, which is a serum called FuegoGrow, and I need you to hear the actual slogan." She read it from the screen. "Regrows your hairline in thirty days or your money back." She looked up. "The comments are insane. He did a countdown, he did a livestream, he cried a little, which, respect, that's craft. By nine o'clock the site said SOLD OUT on two of the five."

"Sold out of how many?"

"That's the thing. Nobody knows. Sold out of a thousand? Of two hundred? Of forty? A number nobody can see isn't a number, it's a costume." She pocketed the phone. "Can I ask the general question? Not about anybody. In general. Regrows your hairline in thirty days. Can a person just say that, about a bottle of anything?"

"No," I said. "A person cannot."

"Then how is it up?"

"Because the people who cannot say it are very often the last to find out, and the finding out does not come from a form letter on day one. It comes later, and it comes with a caseload behind it, and by then the sentence has been printed on everything the person owns." I looked at the amber bottle on the corner of my desk, unlabeled, patient, nine years quiet. "Somewhere in this city, Alexa, there is a woman whose product may have earned that sentence honestly, from a customer who wept when she said it, and she is not allowed to print it either. The law draws its lines where they protect most people, and it does not stop to ask who deserved to stand on which side."

"That's not fair."

"It is not fair. It is merely wise, and on Monday you can have the whole argument, because on Monday I have to explain to a family why the truest thing their customers ever said about them is the one sentence their label can never carry." I closed the file on my desk. "Before that, though, there is a company to build. Papers, owners, percentages. The unglamorous chapter."

Alexa was already at the door. "How hard can that be?" she said. "It's family."

I let that one go where it wanted to go. She would find out soon enough that those two sentences have started more wars than oil.

CHAPTER FIVE

Partners, Paper, and the People We Love

We built the company on paper in a single morning, and it nearly died ten days later at a Sunday dinner I did not attend.

The morning came first. María and Camila sat across from me with the interview findings between them like a settled treaty, and I opened the meeting with a sentence I have delivered so many times that I know where every family flinches.

"Today we decide who owns what, and we decide it while everyone at this table still loves each other, because that condition is temporary in every company ever formed, and paper is the only thing that survives it."

"We already know who owns what," María said. "It is mine and Camila's. Seventy and thirty, like you suggested. What is there to fight about?"

"Today, nothing. That is exactly why today is the day. Señora, before we draw a single percentage, I need to say something formally, because the two of you are two different people even though you share a kitchen. I can help you build this company together while your interests point the same direction. If the day ever comes when they point in different directions, between mother and daughter, each of you may need her own lawyer, and I will be the first to say so out loud. Do you both understand and accept that?"

They looked at each other mildly offended on each other's behalf and accepted.

So, we built it. A Florida limited liability company, which I explained the way I explain it to every family, as a wall. On one side of the wall lives the company, with its bottles, its bank account, its contracts, and its mistakes. On the other side lives everything else, the apartment, the savings, the tuition money, the life. If a batch goes wrong someday, if a delivery van meets a lawsuit, if a contract turns hostile, the damage is meant to stop at the wall. The wall only works if you respect it yourself, one bank account for the company and one for the family, never mixed, but that discipline costs nothing and buys everything.

Then the operating agreement, which is where the real architecture lives, and I made them slow down for every wall and window of it. Seventy percent to María, thirty to Camila, written in numbers nobody would ever have to remember or debate. María as manager, because the maker decides, with Camila's signature required beside her mother's signature for anything above five thousand dollars, because the accountant checks the maker. What happens if a member dies, so that an interest passes inside the family instead of into chaos? What happens if a member divorces, so that a percentage of the company never becomes furniture in someone else's property fight. What happens if the two of them ever deadlock, and what the price of goodbye would be, calculated by a formula they chose now, calmly, instead of screaming across a kitchen later.

"This is morbid," Camila said, somewhere around the death provisions.

"This is love with a notary," I said. "Morbid is doing it afterward. Now, the last piece, and it is the piece I care about most." I set down the pen. "The formula does not go into the company."

They both looked up.

"The company is where the risk lives. Trucks, contracts, batches, lawsuits. You do not store the crown jewels in the room where the fighting happens. The secret stays with María, personally, exactly where it has lived for three generations, and the company receives written permission to use it. A license. If the company ever stumbles, the thing that makes it valuable is not lying on the floor of the building that fell. There is a larger architecture behind that sentence, and one day, when there is more to protect, we will build all of it. Today, the license is enough."

María absorbed this the way she absorbed most things, slowly and completely. "The company borrows the formula," she said. "From me. Like the salons borrow shelf space."

"Better said than I said it, señora."

It was Camila who brought up the name, because the state requires the wall to be called something, and she had her forty candidates open before I finished the sentence. I stopped her.

"Not those names. Those names are the brand, and the brand is next Saturday, and it deserves its own afternoon with its own trapdoors. Today the company needs a legal name the way a filing cabinet needs a label. Boring is fine. Boring is even good."

María thought for a moment, and then she said, quietly, "Restrepo e Hija." Restrepo and Daughter. "If it is going to be boring, it can at least be true."

Camila did not say anything for a second, which for Camila was a paragraph. Then she typed it, and Restrepo e Hija, LLC, went to Tallahassee, and a company that had existed for nine years finally existed.

At the door, gathering her purse, María paused. "And Edgar? He should have something, no? After everything."

"He should have exactly what the three of us design for him this week, on paper, before anyone speaks to him," I said. "Señora, listen to me carefully, because this is the conversation families skip. Choose your partners the way you choose your suppliers, for judgment and conduct, not for love and proximity. Love is why Edgar gets a serious offer. It is not a percentage. Nine years of Saturdays earn gratitude, a real job, real pay, and a real bonus that honors the past. Ownership is a different thing entirely. Ownership is never earned by helping. It is only ever created by agreement, in writing, with numbers in it. So, we will write his offer this week, generously, and we will present it properly, and until then, please, not a word."

"Of course," María said. "Not a word."

* *

She told him at Sunday dinner.

She told me about it afterward, sitting in my office with her hands around a coffee she never drank, and I will tell you the way she told it to me. There had been *sancocho*, and Reina's flan, and Edgar carving at the head of the table the way he had since her mother died, and María had looked at him across all those years of Saturdays and simply could not hold a happy secret in front of family. So, she raised a glass and said the company was real now, official, with papers, and that of course Edgar would be part of it, because they had done it together.

Edgar had stood up and embraced her and wept a little, and then he had tapped his glass and announced to the table that he and María were partners now, fifty and fifty, the way it should be, the way it had always really been.

And María, with the whole family watching, with Reina's flan half served, had said nothing.

"I could not correct him at the table," she told me. "In front of everyone. His birthday is in that same week, *Licenciado.* So, I smiled. And now he has told half of Miami."

I did not say what I could have said, which is that I had asked for one week of silence and received four days. There are moments for the lecture and moments for the tourniquet, and a lawyer who cannot tell them apart helps no one. "Then we meet him this week," I said, "before the story hardens any further. Here, formally, with the offer on paper. And señora, you should know exactly what I am in that room. I am the company's lawyer, and yours. I am not his, and I will say so to his face, and he will have every right to take our offer to a lawyer of his own. If this is done with respect, it can still end at a dinner table instead of a courtroom."

"Edgar would never," she said, and stopped, because the sentence families always say is *he would never*, and she had watched enough of my face by then to know how that sentence ages.

* *

Edgar came on Thursday in his church clothes, which told me everything about what this meeting was to him before he said a word.

He was sixty, built like the work he had done all his life, and he shook my hand with the formality of a man entering enemy territory politely. I told him, first and clearly, that I represented María and the company, not him, that nothing I said was advice to him, and that he was free then and at any moment to have his own lawyer review anything we put in front of him. He waved it away with two fingers.

"Family does not need referees," he said. "Say what you are going to say."

María said it, because I had insisted the offer come from her voice and not from a lawyer's. She had written it out and practiced it, and it was, by any honest measure, generous. A real position, head of distribution, with a salary that matches the work. A signing bonus of ten thousand dollars, in writing, in recognition of nine years of Saturdays, the table he built, the van, the festivals at four in the morning. First right to grow with the company as it grows. All of it on two pages, in plain language, next to one more page that released the past so both sides could stand on clean ground.

Edgar listened with his hands flat on my conference table. When she finished, he was quiet for a long moment, and when he finally spoke, his voice was not angry, which was worse.

"Nine years," he said. "I never asked you for a receipt, María. Not for gas, not for the van, not for my Saturdays. When the table broke at the church, I built another one that same week with my own wood. When your mother was sick, who drove? And now the company is real, and there is a lawyer, and there are papers, and what the papers say is that I am an employee." He pushed the pages back an inch with one finger. "A salary. In my own family's company. You are offering to pay me for what I gave."

"Edgar," María said, "the bonus, the position, it is real, it is written, we made it before—"

"I do not want to be paid, María. I want to be counted." He stood, and he buttoned his church jacket, and the terrible thing was his composure. "You know what your mother would say. Family does not sign papers with family. The signing is the insult. Not the numbers. I would have taken any numbers, if they had come with the word *socio* in front of them." Partner. He looked at me without hostility, the way you look at weather. "No offense to you, Doctor. You did your work. This is what your work does to families."

He did not slam the door. He closed it, gently, which took longer and said more, and through the glass wall of the conference room I watched him cross the lobby past an older couple waiting on the sofa, past the front desk, where my niece had stopped typing, and out.

Nobody spoke for a moment. Then María asked the question quietly, in the voice people use for asking about tumors. "Can he do something? Legally. Against us."

"I will answer that honestly, because you have earned honest answers. There is no paper anywhere with his name on it, and that cuts both ways. It means he owns nothing. It also means the story of those nine years has no written ending, and a man with no written ending can, if he ever chooses, walk into a courtroom and ask it to write one, with words like partnership and promises. Would he win? Almost certainly not. Would it cost this family money and two years of Sunday dinners to find out? Yes. That is what the release on page three was for, and it is the page he did not sign." I gathered the offer back into its folder, and I did not close the folder. "So here is what we do. The offer stays open. We put nothing in writing to him that is not kind. And from today, everything this company does gets documented as it happens, so that the next nine years, unlike the last nine, will be able to speak for themselves."

María looked at the folder for a long time. "Keep it in the file," she said. "The whole offer. Exactly as it is. In case he ever..." She did not finish it, and I did not make her.

* *

The older couple from the lobby sofa were my eleven o'clock, and they had seen everything a lobby lets you see, which is the shape of a fight without its words.

They were Silvia and Diego Ferraro, from Buenos Aires, thirty-four years married, twenty-two years in this country, and they ran a small salon in Westchester where, for special clients, Silvia mixed a rinse that made gray hair surrender. Her mother's formula. Her grandmother's before that. Diego, over two decades of salon work, had perfected how it was applied, the timing and the technique, so that the recipe was hers and the method was his and the customers were theirs, and none of it was written anywhere, and both of them knew every word of it by heart.

They sat close together on the same side of my desk, the way long-married couples do, and Silvia came at it sideways, in the *porteño* way, watching me over her glasses.

"The gentleman who left," she said. "*Mirá*, we could not hear anything, and we did not try. But we have eyes, *viste*. A man in his best clothes, leaving a lawyer's office slowly." She folded her hands. "Diego and I talked about it right there on your sofa, and we decided to say to you what we said to each other. That man had no paper. And neither do we."

"Thirty-four years," Diego said. It was nearly the only thing he said in the whole meeting, and he said it like a man setting down something heavy. "Her recipe. My hands. No paper."

"We are not afraid of each other," Silvia said quickly, touching his arm. "After thirty-four years, if we were going to kill each other, we would have done it during the World Cup. But we watched that man walk out, and I thought, we are two people who own one secret, and we have never once asked the question. If Diego is gone tomorrow, God forbid, what do I own? If I am gone, what does he own? If, God forbid twice, the marriage ever broke, who keeps my grandmother? There are no children in the salon, *Licenciado*. There is no one after us who knows it. It all lives in two heads that sleep in one bed, and this morning your lobby taught us that love is not a filing system."

I looked at the two of them, and at the amber bottle in its corner, and I thought about how a single Thursday can arrange itself into a lesson no one planned.

"Señora Ferraro," I said, "you have just described your situation more precisely than most clients manage after three meetings, so I will match your honesty. You are right to be here, you are early enough for everything, and the questions you asked have real answers, all of them buildable. But we start where every family starts in this office." I took out a fresh legal pad. "Four pages. Handwritten, in whatever language they arrive."

* *

María and Camila signed the operating agreement the following Tuesday, at four in the afternoon, at my conference table, with the third chair empty.

Nobody mentioned the chair. Camila signed the way she did everything, fast and exact, and then María took the pen, and I noticed, because it is my job to notice, that she had brought her own. A blue ballpoint, worn at the grip. She signed Restrepo e Hija into existence in her mother's ink, seventy and thirty, license and all, and when she finished, she looked not at the agreement but at the folder on the corner of my desk, the one that stayed open.

"Now there is a paper that says who we are," she said. "I used to think that was a cold thing. A paper like that." She capped the pen. "It is not cold. It is just early. That is all it is. Everything with Edgar came nine years too late, so it burned. This one comes on time."

On Saturday, Camila would arrive with her forty names, and I would have to teach two women who had just survived a war over what was unwritten that the next war is over what gets written, because names have trapdoors, and Spanish names have more of them, and family surnames, which was all either of my client families had ever wanted to put on a label, have the deepest trapdoors of all.

CHAPTER SIX
The Name They Fell in Love With

Camila arrived at the naming meeting with a secret of her own, which in this family was becoming a tradition.

She set her laptop on the conference table, and next to it she set an amber bottle, and the bottle had a label on it. It was a real one, printed on her home printer, trimmed with scissors, and taped on with the family's traditional material. She turned the bottle to face her mother, not me, and on the label, in handwriting I recognized before I understood why, was a single word.

MARTICA.

María made a sound I had not heard from her in six weeks of meetings, a small sound, mostly breath, and put her hand flat against her chest.

"In Medellín, nobody called her Marta," Camila said, quietly, watching her mother. "You told me that. The neighbors, the salon, everybody said Martica. Only the bank called her Marta." She touched the label. "And this is her actual handwriting. I scanned the tape from your notebook, the FORTALECEDOR strip, and I rebuilt the letters she didn't write, matching her hand. It took me all night." She turned the bottle a few degrees, the way you angle a photograph of someone who has died. "Forty names, Profe. I ranked them for six days. And then at two in the morning, I realized number one was never on the list, because she was in the kitchen the whole time."

The room did what rooms do around that kind of moment. María took the bottle in both hands. She traced the M with her thumb. She said her mother's nickname once, in the voice people use in churches, and then she looked at me with her whole face already decided, and said, "This one, *Licenciado*. This is the name. I do not need to see the other thirty-nine."

And this is the exact moment, in every naming story I have ever been part of, where trouble begins, and it never begins in the choosing. It begins in the order of the choosing. Because love had now been spent, a night of work had been spent, a dead woman's handwriting had been resurrected and taped to a bottle, and no one at that table had yet asked the only question the law cares about, which is not whether the name is beautiful, but whether the name is free.

I did not take the moment from them. I have learned that much in twenty years. I let María hold the bottle, and I let Camila have her mother's face, and then I said, as gently as the sentence can be said, "It is a beautiful name, and tonight I am going to try to find out who else owns it."

Camila's head came up. "Who else? It's my grandmother's nickname."

"It is also, forgive me, a name thousands of grandmothers have answered to, and we are not asking whether your family loves it. We are asking whether the United States trademark system has already promised it to someone else. So, before anything else, let me do what I should have insisted on doing before you opened that laptop, and what I want you to remember for the rest of your lives in business. First the search. Then the falling in love. In that order, always, because the heart does not read the trademark register, and the register does not care what the heart has already spent."

* *

The other thirty-nine died faster than Camila expected, and the manner of their dying was itself the afternoon's education, because her list, without knowing it, had wandered into every trap the trademark office sets for families like this one.

"CRECEPELO," I read. Grows hair. "Dead twice. Once because a name that merely describes what a product does is the weakest kind of mark there is, so weak the law may refuse to let anyone own it at all. And once because of what the two of you learned three weeks ago. A name that promises to grow hair is not just a weak trademark. It is a drug claim printed on the front of the bottle, permanently, in your own chosen letters. SEDOSA, silky. Descriptive, weak, and half the shampoo aisle already whispers it. And before either of you objects that these words are in Spanish, hear the rule that surprises everyone. The trademark office translates. It is called the doctrine of foreign equivalents. A Spanish word is examined through its English meaning, so FORTALECEDOR is judged as STRENGTHENER, and CRECEPELO is judged as HAIR GROWER, and the language of your grandmother gives you no hiding place. They translate the weakness."

"Wait." Camila had stopped scrolling. "So, the government translates our Spanish when it hurts us. Do the customers get it translated when it helps us? Does Marisol's trust translate?"

"Write that question down, because it is a better question than most lawyers ever ask, and the honest answer is no. The doctrine translates your words. Nobody translates your goodwill. That you have to carry across the bridge yourself, and we will talk about the bridge before you leave. Now. RESTREPO." I tapped the screen. "Here is the trap I have been waiting for two client families to spring. The law is suspicious of surnames. A mark that is primarily merely a surname is refused, ordinarily, until years of use teaches the public that the word means your product and not just somebody's family. Restrepo is a common name. Ten thousand Restrepos would like a word with you about who owns it. The rule softens for rare surnames, and I happened to be walking a client through that exact softness this same month, a man whose surname almost nobody in this country carries, which changes the mathematics entirely. But Restrepo is not rare, and the refusal writes itself. MEDELLÍN. ANTIOQUIA. Place names, and place names carry two different trapdoors, one for each direction of the truth. If the product actually comes from the place, the name merely describes its origin, and descriptive is weak. If the product does not come from the place, and yours is made in a kitchen in Miami, then the name is worse than weak. It suggests an origin that is false, and the law has a special refusal for geography that lies."

Camila looked at her murdered list for a while. "So Spanish words get translated against us. Our own last name is suspicious. And the city we're actually from is either weak or a lie." She sat back. "The system was not built for us, Profe."

"The system was built for buyers," I said, "to make sure a name on a shelf tells them the truth about where a thing comes from, and once you understand that you can make the system work harder for this family than it ever worked against it. Because there is a whole category your list barely touched. Invented words. Borrowed words that have nothing to do with hair. Names that describe nothing, promise nothing, and therefore can belong to you completely. The strongest names in the world are the ones that meant nothing until the product taught people what they meant. Nobody knew what a Kodak was. Now, the survivors." Three names remained, and MARTICA stood at the top of them, taped to a bottle, written in a dead woman's hand. "The survivors go to the search. Knockout tonight, the full search this week. Camila, until the results come back, the label stays in this office, and nothing gets printed, posted, ordered, or whispered to a salon. We do not introduce a name to the market until we know the market is allowed to keep it."

* *

The results came back on Thursday, and I have delivered worse news in that conference room, but rarely to a quieter table.

"MARTIKA," I said, and spelled it. "With a K. Registered eleven years ago, for hair care preparations, exactly your category. The owner is a company in New Jersey, the registration is alive and maintained, and their products are in stores. I am sorry. The name is taken."

"It's not the same name," Camila said instantly. "Theirs has a K. Ours has a C. It's spelled differently. It's one letter, and we can—"

"Say them both out loud."

She did not say them, because she had already heard it. Spoken aloud, Martica and Martika are one word, and the law knows what the mouth knows. "Trademarks are compared the way customers actually meet them," I said. "By sound, by appearance, by meaning, by the impression they leave. A woman tells her sister on the telephone, buy the Martica one, and the sister comes home with theirs. That is the entire test, and we failed it in one breath. One letter is not a moat, *mija*. One letter is a costume."

"Then we add a word. Martica Original. Casa Martica. We fight for it. You said the office refuses things. Fine. We argue. People argue with the government all the time. You're a lawyer. That's the whole—"

"Camila." María had not spoken since the spelling. She reached over and closed the laptop, softly, the way she did most final things. "*Mija.* Stop. Listen to what you are saying. Three weeks ago, a man stood in that lobby in his church clothes because nobody made the papers in time. Now the papers came first, they came back, and they said no, and you want to argue with the paper because you love the name." She took her daughter's hand. "I love it too. I held the bottle and I heard my mother's kitchen. But your uncle taught you the words for this in the first week, and I have been waiting to see if you would say them to yourself." She smiled a little. "It is a beautiful door, *mija.* It is locked."

I gave the silence its time. Then I gave them the honest map, because grief deserves a map. "There are paths to fight for a taken name, and I will name them, so you know I am not hiding them. You can ask the owner for a written consent, which costs money and begs a competitor for permission to exist. You can hunt their registration for weaknesses, which is war, and war is for assets worth a war. Or you can crowd next to them unregistered and hope, which builds your family's future on another company's patience. Every one of those paths spends years and money to end up sharing a name. Or." I turned the amber bottle on my desk, the unlabeled one, the original, so that the window light went through it. "You can remember that the thing you actually loved was never the letters."

Camila looked at the bottle for a long moment. "The handwriting," she said. "The handwriting was the part that made Mamá cry. Abuela isn't in the name. She's in the hand."

"So, keep the hand. The handwriting, the amber glass, the strip of tape that this family has been using as a label for thirty years without knowing it was a design. All of that is yours, it does not belong to anyone else, and the law protects the look and feel of a package too, when the look is distinctive, and I promise you no factory in New Jersey has your grandmother's penmanship. The story survives. It just needs a free name to carry it." I nudged the bottle an inch toward them. "And you have both been staring at it for six weeks."

María saw it first. She picked up the bottle, and she said the color out loud, in Spanish, the way she would have said it to a customer. "*Ámbar.*"

"Ambarina," Camila said. Almost immediately, the way she did everything. Then again, listening to it. "Ambarina. Little amber. It's barely even a word. It describes nothing and it promises nothing." She looked up at me, already knowing. "Which is the point. That's the whole point, isn't it? It means nothing yet."

"It means nothing yet," I said, "which in this building is the most valuable thing a name can mean. Because a name that means nothing is an empty vessel, and this family happens to own nine years of something to pour into it."

* *

The searches on AMBARINA came back clean the following week, and then we did the thing that this entire chapter of their lives had been building toward, and it took eleven minutes.

We filed for the trademark before the first bottle bearing it was ever sold. The law allows exactly this, an application built on a sworn, genuine intent to use the name in commerce, and it plants your flag in the national register while your labels are still being designed. From the day of filing, the family's place in line was fixed. Anyone who came later, with any spelling, in any language, would find Restrepo e Hija already standing there. I told them there was a wider world of flags, other countries, the places Marisol ships bottles to, and that those filings would have their moment when the company was ready to feed them. One flag first. The right flag, in the right ground, at the right time.

Camila redesigned the label that same night, because of course she did. She brought it in the next morning, taped to the bottle in the traditional material: AMBARINA in Marta's reconstructed hand, on amber glass, over a thin printed strip made to look like masking tape, and below it, small and in ordinary type, the truthful words the salons could keep saying out loud for free: *el de Doña María.*

María held it at arm's length, then close, then at arm's length again, the way women of her generation read menus, and what she finally said, she said to the label and not to us.

"My mother sold this her whole life with a word that described it," she said. "Now it has a name that belongs to it." She set the bottle on my desk, next to its unlabeled twin, the original, and the two of them stood there together, before and after, nine years apart. "Bueno. The name has papers. The company has papers." She gathered her purse, and at the door she turned, and her face had the look it gets when she is about to hand me the next mountain. "So now, *Licenciado*, we must talk about the part I have been avoiding since the first day. If we are going to grow, I cannot make two hundred bottles alone in my kitchen forever. Which means the formula must finally be written down, completely, for someone else's hands. And you are going to tell me who is allowed to hold the paper." She said it lightly, but her thumb was moving over the strap of her purse. "Luz has been asking why I am so quiet lately. She was at Camila's baptism, *Licenciado*. And you are going to make me ask my *comadre* to sign."

"Señora," I said, "I am going to teach you how to build a fence. Who stands inside it is a conversation for people who love each other, and it will be the hardest paper this family signs all year."

She nodded, because she already knew, and the door closed, and the two amber bottles stood on my desk in the afternoon light, the named and the nameless, and somewhere across town a man with a group chat for a confidentiality program had just received his first email from a lawyer who was not his.

PART III

THE FORMULA

CHAPTER SEVEN
Behind the Fence

The formula was written down for the first time in three generations on a Tuesday afternoon, in María's kitchen, with the blinds closed, and I was not there, and neither was anyone else.

That was the architecture, and we had drawn it together the week before, at my conference table, before a single word went on paper. Because here is the thing nobody tells a family about writing down the sacred recipe. The writing is the easy part. The hard part is that the moment a secret becomes a document, it becomes a thing that can be copied, photographed, borrowed, and stolen, and so the fence has to exist before the treasure does.

"Start with what the fence does not protect," I told them, "because it will save you from guarding the wrong gate. One day soon, the law is going to require the ingredients printed on every label you sell. Every competitor, every chemist, every curious stranger will be able to read the nouns of your formula off the shelf for the price of one bottle. That is not a catastrophe. That is the rule for everyone, and it is why the ingredient list was never the secret. The secret is everything the shelf cannot say. The amounts. The order. The timing. The temperatures. The waiting, and how long, and how you know when it is done. The supplier, and the grade, and why that source and no other. A stranger with your ingredient list has nouns. Your family owns the verbs and the numbers, and the fence we build protects those."

So, the document itself was built like a fence, in two parts that were never to live together. One page held the identities and the sources. A second held the amounts, the sequence, and the waiting. Alone, each page was a torso without a head. Together, they were the inheritance, and together happened nowhere except inside María, and now inside a safe-deposit box, in two numbered envelopes, in her own hand, written alone in a kitchen with the blinds closed.

"And copies?" Camila asked.

"Numbered, counted, and boring. Every copy that ever exists gets a number and a name attached to it, in a log, and the log is the first thing we read if there is ever trouble. A secret is not a possession. It is a practice, and the practice is mostly lists."

Then I slid the last page across the table, and it was the shortest one, and it was the one María had been dreading since the day she told me who helped on the big days.

It was a list of every person who would ever stand inside the fence, and what each of them was permitted to know, and next to each name, a line for a signature. It worked in tiers, like the levels of a house. Camila would hold most of it, as she had always known it. A manufacturer, someday, would hold some of it, under paper we had not written yet. And then there was Luz. Her tier was simply the truth of the last nine years, written down and given walls: the steps, never the amounts, plus a promise, in Spanish and English in two columns on one page, that what she saw in that kitchen stayed in that kitchen, forever, no matter what happened between the families.

María looked at the signature line for a long time.

"Half of Miami already says I made Edgar sign papers," she said. "Now I ask my *comadre*. *Licenciado*, Luz held Camila at the baptism. She stood before God with me. And I am going to hand her a paper with a line on it."

"Then hand it to her the way it deserves," I said. "Not here. Not from me. At her table or yours, from your own hands, with the truth. And señora, take her this, because it is the part nobody hears the first time. That signature is not a fence against Luz. It is a roof over her. The day something ever goes wrong, the day the formula turns up where it should not be, every person near this family will be a question mark except the ones with signatures. The paper is not suspicion. The paper is the end of suspicion, in advance, forever. A person inside the fence can never be accused of climbing it."

María took the page. She folded it the way she folded final things, in half and then in half again, and she put it in her purse, and she said, "She refused Edgar's daughter a loan once and brought her a stove instead. I know my *comadre*, *Licenciado*. She will understand."

She was wrong, and I think part of her knew it walking out, because love makes excellent maps of everything except itself.

* *

Luz refused on a Sunday, in her own kitchen, with the coffee already served, which in that world is the most serious possible venue for a no.

María told me about it on Monday, sitting very straight, describing it the way people describe car accidents, in the order things broke. She had done everything right: the visit, the truth, the roof and not the fence, her own hands. And Luz had listened to all of it with the page in front of her, untouched, next to the coffee, and then she had said the thing that had nothing to do with the page.

"She said, *comadre*, you went quiet on me five weeks ago." María's voice stayed level with effort. "She said, the paper is not the insult. The paper is the confession. You built the fence weeks ago, María, I have been standing outside it since before the lawyer printed the line for my name. Forty years, and you let an office into the kitchen before you let me back in." María looked at her hands. "And then she said Edgar was right about one thing. Not the fifty percent. He was a fool about the fifty percent. But he said the signing is the insult, and *comadre*, look at us. He was not entirely a fool."

"And the page?"

"On the table. Next to the coffee. She did not tear it. She did not touch it." María folded her hands. "With us, *Licenciado*, that is worse."

I want to record what I told her then, because it is the conversation I believe in most and enjoy least. "Señora, you now have a choice, and it is the real one, the one this whole month has been walking toward. Luz can stand in your kitchen on the big days unsigned, the way she always has, and the odds are good that nothing bad ever happens, because she loves you, and love is real. Or the fence holds for everyone, including the person it hurts most to hold it against, and you pay for that on Sundays.

I will not pretend the second choice is free. I will only tell you what I have seen in twenty years. A fence with one gap in it for love is not a fence with a gap. It is a gap with a story, and every future person you ever ask to sign, every manufacturer, every employee, every partner, will learn that the rule bent once, for someone, and rules that bend for someone are rules that negotiate."

María was quiet for a long time. "The big order from the salons comes in two weeks," she said. "Three hundred bottles. I cannot do three hundred without her."

"Yes, you can," I said. "It will just cost what it costs."

It cost a rescheduled midterm, two fourteen-hour Saturdays, a burn on Camila's wrist the size of a peso, and a month of Sundays with an empty chair at a second table, so that María's family now had two wounds where its gatherings used to be. They made the three hundred bottles, the two of them alone, with the radio off because María could not stand the ballads that month. The fence held. I never said it was painless. I said it was a fence.

* *

That same week, a woman from São Paulo taught my office what the far side of the fence looks like.

Her name was Juliana, she did keratin, and she arrived the way weather arrives, all at once and talking. She had heard from a stylist who had heard from a salon that there was a lawyer who helped people like her, and she had a treatment, *querida*, not like the others, a smoothing system she had developed herself over six years, gentler, cleverer, hers, and she wanted to do what smart people do, she wanted to protect it.

I did with her what I now do with everyone, which is that before we discussed what to build, we audited what was already standing, and I asked the question I had learned to ask early. "Juliana, before today, where has the method ever appeared outside your own hands? Interviews, videos, classes, posts. Anything public, ever."

She waved this away, and then she stopped waving, and I watched a memory arrive on her face like a bill.

"There was one interview," she said. "Two years ago. A Brazilian beauty channel, very respected, *meu Deus*, eighty thousand views. I was so proud, you understand, nobody from my neighborhood gets asked. They filmed in my salon. I demonstrated everything." She looked at me with the beginning of the correct fear. "I said the ratios, *Licenciado*. On camera. I was showing that I was generous. In my community, the ones who hide everything are the ones with nothing."

We found it in four minutes, because everything is four minutes away now. There she was, two years younger, luminous, holding two bottles to the lens, telling eighty thousand strangers the exact proportions, and I let her watch thirty seconds of it before I stopped it, because there is no lecture equal to a person's own face saying the numbers out loud.

"Now hear the two halves of your situation, because you came for the truth and both halves are true. The first half is hard. A secret that has been told is not a secret, and the law will not pretend otherwise. What you said on that camera belongs to the world now. It cannot be recalled, relicensed, or resented back into the vault. And understand something colder. Even without the video, the law permits any competitor to buy your product, take it to a laboratory, and figure out whatever the product itself can be made to confess. That is called reverse engineering, and it is legal, and it is honest work in the law's eyes. The shelf betrays. The camera betrays faster. Neither is theft."

Juliana had gone very still, which I suspected was rare.

"The second half is the reason you are not leaving this office in despair. A hole in the fence is a hole. It is not the removal of the fence. Tell me. In the two years since that interview, has the method changed? Improved? Adjusted?"

"*Querida*," she said, offended into her old self for a second, "I improve it every six months. The ratios in that video are two generations old. My supplier changed. My timing changed. The finishing step is completely new. Nobody has seen—"

She stopped herself, midsentence, with her own hand almost rising, and I watched a woman who had spent her life being generous with knowledge feel, for the first time, the instinct María had shown in her first ten minutes.

"Good," I said. "Hold that feeling. That is the fence, arriving. What you gave away is gone, and what you have built since is yours, and from today it gets walls. Everything from this moment forward, the current ratios, the new supplier, the finishing step you nearly just performed for a lawyer, lives behind paper. Four pages first. You know what to write, and what not to."

"The lady with the amber bottle did the four pages too?" she asked, gathering her enormous bag. Word travels in salons the way it travels nowhere else on earth.

"Everyone does the four pages," I said, and did not answer the rest.

* *

Victor, meanwhile, had gone to war on camera, because for Victor there was no other place to go.

Alexa showed me at the end of the day, phone flat on my desk, with the expression she reserves for slow-motion film of bridge collapsing. He had received a letter, the one whose arrival closed the last chapter, and it turned out to be exactly what launching five products under an uncleared name earns a man. A company that had owned a registered mark with the word Fuego in it, for cosmetics, for a decade, had written him the polite-artillery letter lawyers write. And Victor had responded by reading it aloud to his followers, live, waving the pages, announcing that a corporation was trying to steal his brand, the brand he built with his bare hands, and that he did not negotiate with bullies.

"He's turning a cease-and-desist into content," Alexa said. "The comments are calling him brave." She watched a few more seconds. "You made me sign a confidentiality agreement on my first morning here. Day one, before coffee. You know what I felt? Hired. I felt like what I was going to hear mattered." She picked the phone back up. "A month ago,

I would have told you Victor's way looks like winning. Now I watch him wave that letter and all I can think of is, he has no idea what it costs, because nobody ever made him sign anything, because nobody ever trusted him with anything worth a signature."

I wrote that down myself, in my own notebook, because some tuition arrives from unexpected directions.

* *

Luz came to my office in the fifth week, uninvited, carrying Tupperware, because she was constitutionally incapable of arriving anywhere with empty hands, even into battle.

"You are the man," she said, sitting down and placing the container on my desk like a subpoena, "who is teaching my *comadre* that forty years needs a signature."

I have been cross-examined by professionals. Luz was better, because she had no rules of procedure and total moral jurisdiction. I let her empty all of it onto my desk: the five silent weeks, the gossip about Edgar with her brother's name in every retelling, the evening she learned there was a lawyer before she learned there was a fence, and the empty chair that was her own chair, at a table she had helped cook for since before Camila existed. I did not defend a word of it, because most of it did not deserve defending, and I told her so, plainly, and something in her recalibrated when I did.

"The silence was wrong," I said. "María knows it, and it happened on my watch, so some of it is mine. You are also right that the paper came late and cold, after the distance instead of before it. Everything you have said is true, señora. Now let me say one thing that is also true. You stood at a baptism once and made promises out loud, before God, about a child who was not yours. Nobody in that church called the promises an insult to your love. The promises were the love, spoken where it counted, in front of the witness that mattered. That is all this page is. The same family, making the same kind of promise about the other thing it inherited, in front of the witness that matters for inheritances, which in this country, señora, is the law. Not because love failed. Because love, in this family, finally has something that will outlive it."

Luz looked at me for a long moment. Then she looked at the amber bottles on the corner of my desk, the named one and the nameless one, and whatever argument she had brought in the Tupperware, she left there.

"I will sign," she said, standing, straightening her blouse the way generals straighten uniforms. "But not here. Papers of an office get signed in an office. Papers of a family get signed at the stove." She pointed at me on her way to the door. "And you will tell María that I take the big days back, all of them, and that she owes me five Sundays, and that if she ever goes quiet on me again, no paper in Florida will protect her."

She signed that Saturday at María's kitchen table, both columns, Spanish and English, with the pots already warming behind her, and Camila told me later that the radio was back on, and that the three of them made ninety bottles before dark, and that her mother sang.

I put Luz's page in the log, copy number four, and I noted the date, because the ledger does not record singing, and somebody should. And underneath the log, in the same file, sat a different page waiting for its own chapter, the one María had surrendered almost shyly during the writing-down, torn from her private notes and labeled in her round hand, *cosas para después*. Things for later. On it, sketched in pencil, was an idea her mother had never imagined, a bottle in two chambers, the phases kept apart until the moment of use, never built, never sold, never spoken outside a kitchen with the blinds closed.

Its history was perfectly clean, and so the election her original formula never got to make was waiting, patiently, for the one thing this family had finally invented on this side of the border. The choice would be the loud door or the silent one, and in two weeks, at a table in Doral, a truck driver with a redesigned mixing method was going to face the exact same fork.

CHAPTER EIGHT
The Election You Cannot Undo

María unfolded the pencil sketch on my conference table, smoothed it flat with both hands, and told me what she wanted before I could say a word about what she had.

"I want the word, *Licenciado.*" She tapped the drawing of the two-chambered bottle, the phases kept apart until the moment of use, the idea her mother never imagined. "Patented. On the label, in English, where Marisol's daughter can read it. *Patente americana.* My mother sold from a folding table her whole life, and nothing she ever made had had a paper with a seal on it. This one will."

I have heard that want in a hundred accents, and I have learned to respect it before I complicate it, because it is not vanity. For a family that crossed a border with its wealth stored in a grandmother's memory, a government document with a number on it is not decoration. It is arrival. So, I did not begin with the price. I began with the promise, and then I made them stay for the whole contract.

"Then let me tell you exactly what the word costs, señora, because a patent is a trade, and I have watched people choose wrongly in both directions across this table. Here is the deal the government offers. You teach the world, completely and in public, how to make and use your invention. Not a summary. A lesson so complete that a stranger could build it from your pages alone, and if you hold back the clever part, the whole thing can die for the holding back. In exchange, you receive roughly twenty years, counted from the day you file, in which no one may make it, use it, or sell it without your permission, even a stranger who invents it honestly in his own garage. When the twenty years end, your lesson belongs to everyone, forever. And one more thing, the part that surprises every family. About a year and a half after filing, the application publishes to the world, whether or not a patent is ever granted. The blueprint goes public on schedule. The monopoly is merely an application."

"Twenty years," Camila said, running the arithmetic that ran in her constantly. "The formula is on year, what, sixty? Seventy, counting Abuela's mother?"

"Which is why the formula already made its election, and made it correctly, and nothing about today reopens that door. Today is only about this." I put my finger on the sketch. "And for this, the choice is real, because its history is clean. Never built, never sold, never posted, never whispered. This drawing is standing exactly where your family's original formula stood a hundred years ago, at the fork, with both doors open. So, we choose. And we do not choose by feeling. We choose by asking the invention three questions about itself."

I wrote them on the pad between us.

"First. Does it tell its own secret? Look at your bottle, señora. The moment it sits on a shelf, every customer, every competitor, every chemist with a credit card can see the two chambers, twist the mechanism, and understand the idea by Friday. A design that ships in public view cannot be a secret, because the product itself confesses. For this invention, the silent door is an illusion. It is patent or nothing.

"Second. If someone copies it, would you ever know? Yes. A copied bottle stands on a shelf in daylight, with a barcode, in a store, where your own customers will photograph it for you within a week. A patent is only as good as your ability to catch the infringer, and this invention gets caught by walking past it. That makes the twenty-years enforceable, which makes them worth buying.

"Third. How long does the advantage last? Packaging moves in generations. Twenty years of exclusivity on a mechanism like this is not a limitation. It is probably longer than the mechanism's whole commercial life. The clock that terrifies me for a seventy-year formula is generous for a bottle."

María was watching the sketch. "And the formula fails all three."

"The formula passes the opposite test on all three, which is why it lives behind the fence. It does not confess itself, because the shelf betrays the nouns and keeps the verbs. Infringement of a recipe happens inside a stranger's factory where you would never see it. And its useful life is measured in generations, not product cycles. Same family, two inventions, opposite doors, and both answers correct. That, señora, is the whole discipline. Not every treasure goes in the same vault."

"So, we file," María said, and her chin came up half an inch. "And the label says patented."

"The label will say Patent Pending, and it will say it honestly, and soon, and I will explain the difference in a moment. But first." I turned to Camila, because I had seen the laptop bag, and I had learned to fear content calendars the way sailors fear pretty weather. "Before anything is filed, I need to know what is scheduled."

* *

She had, of course, already made the video.

Camila pulled it up with the wounded efficiency of a person who has prepared a surprise and watched it become evidence. It ran thirty seconds, beautifully cut: her own hands turning a cardboard prototype of the two-chamber bottle in warm light, the masking-tape aesthetic, Marta's reconstructed handwriting, a title card that said INNOVATION HAS AN ACCENT, and a scheduled date eleven days out, timed to build launch buzz.

"It's a teaser," she said. "It doesn't explain anything. It's thirty seconds of a prototype in nice light."

"It is thirty seconds of the invention, in public, on a date certain," I said, "and I want both of you to understand what that post would have done, because this is the sentence this whole chapter of your lives turns on. In this country, an inventor who discloses her own invention gets one year of grace to file, one year, and then the door closes the way it closed on the original formula. But Marisol ships bottles to Barranquilla, señora. You told me so in the first week. And in most of the world, there is no year. There is no grace at all. In Colombia, in Europe, in nearly every market your family will ever care about, the rule is absolute novelty, which means the invention must be new on the day of filing, period. One thirty-second video, and the United States starts a countdown while Colombia simply closes, permanently, eleven days from now, because of lighting and a title card." I let the room hold that. "You would not have decided the election. You would have let the calendar decide it, by default, in favor of nothing."

Camila looked at her own video for a moment, her hands turning the little cardboard bottle in warm light, and then she deleted the scheduled post while we watched, which for Camila was the equivalent of a formal apology with witnesses.

"New rule," she said. "Nothing I make goes public until it goes past you. That's annoying. Write it down anyway."

"It is already in the fence," I said. "You just heard it click."

* *

The search took three weeks, and it did to María's dream what searches do, which is shrink it into something real.

"The world has seen two-chambered bottles," I told them when the results were in. "Dozens of them, going back decades, for cosmetics, for glues, for medicines. If we had filed on the idea of two chambers, the examiner would have buried us politely by return mail. That is not a defeat. That is the map. Because the search also shows what the world has not seen, and it is the part your mother actually invented, señora, the part that came from her problem and nobody else's. The waiting. Every prior bottle mixes and hands the job to the customer. Yours meters the phases to the family's ratio, and it announces its own readiness, and that pairing, the metering matched to the maturation, is where the search runs quiet. So that is where the invention lives, and it is where the claims will live, and I will tell you now the sentence I tell everyone at this stage. The patent you can get is always smaller than the patent you imagined, and it is worth more, because it is real."

Then we did the filing the way the moment deserved, in the right order, with the right paper.

"Today we file what is called a provisional application. Think of it as an anchor. It is quieter and cheaper than the full application, it does not get examined, and it holds your place in line for one year, dated today, while the product finishes becoming itself. From today, this family may print Patent Pending, honestly, on anything the mechanism touches. Within the year we file the full application, the complete lesson, the claims, the real cost, and I will say the numbers out loud now, so they never surprise you. The anchor is modest. The full application and the years of examination behind it will run well into five figures before we are done, and the patent, if granted, charges rent in maintenance fees for its whole life. This is why the three questions come first. You do not buy a twenty-year sword for an invention that could not be enforced or would not be copied. You buy it for this one."

"And the writing," María said. She had been circling something for two meetings, and now she landed on it. "The application teaches the world the bottle. Completely, you said. A lesson a stranger could build from." Her eyes went to the corner of my desk, to the amber bottles, the named and the nameless. "How much of the kitchen goes into the lesson?"

"None of it," I said. "And I am glad you asked it out loud, because this is the discipline inside the discipline. The application will teach the bottle completely and the formula not at all. The mechanism does not care what it meters. So, the pages will speak of a first phase and a second phase, generically, the way an architect draws a safe without listing what the family keeps inside it. The patent gets the machine. The house keeps the kitchen."

María repeated that quietly, in Spanish, to herself, rearranged into something her mother might have said. "*La cocina se queda en la casa. La botella puede salir a la calle.*" The kitchen stays in the house. The bottle can go out to the street. Then she asked me for a copy of the filing receipt, the plain one, with the date and the application number, and she did not explain why, and she did not have to. Some families frame diplomas. Hers was going to frame an anchor.

It was Camila, gathering the laptop, who named what we had built, and she named it in her own language, which was never Spanish or English but accounting.

"You realize what this is now," she said. "It's a portfolio. Three assets, three different clocks. The formula is the land. It doesn't expire, but you have to fence it every single day. The patent is a building on a twenty-year lease, loud and rentable and temporary. And the name is the goodwill line, the only asset that gets *more* valuable every year the other two do their jobs." She zipped the bag. "Land, building, goodwill. Abuela was a balance sheet the whole time. Somebody should have told her."

* *

Carlos made his election the following week, at a *panadería* table in Doral, over coffee he insisted on buying, and he chose the opposite door, and he was right too.

His four pages were immaculate, of course, written like maintenance logs. The invention he had redesigned in his head across six years of night shifts was a method, a way of combining that changed what the cream became, invisible in the finished product, detectable by no one who did not stand inside the room where it happened. I asked his invention the same three questions I had asked María's, out loud, in the same order, and I watched a careful man hear the answers arrive like verdicts he was checking against his own arithmetic.

"It does not confess itself," he said slowly. "You could buy a thousand jars and never see the method. And if a factory in New Jersey used it behind their own walls..." He stopped. "I would never know. My whole life, I would never know. The patent would be, what. A published instruction manual, with my name on it, teaching the men I could never catch." He set down the coffee. "Doctor. I have wanted the certificate since I was thirty years old. It was the plan. First the patent. You are telling me the correct move, for my best invention, is silence."

"I am telling you the correct move is the one the invention asks for, and yours asks for walls, not trumpets. And Don Carlos, hear what silence buys when it is built properly, because it is not the silence you kept in Valencia. There you kept the secret because there was no law worth trusting, so the secret was only as strong as your own locked door. Here the silence gets architecture. Paper, tiers, signatures, a law that punishes the thief instead of shrugging at him. And no clock. A patent on your method would die in twenty years and hand the lesson to everyone at the funeral. The method, fenced, can belong to your grandchildren." I slid one more page across the table, because the week had one piece of loud news in it after all. "And you do not leave empty-handed on the trumpet side. The search on your surname came back. Uzcátegui is rare enough in this country that the objection that buries common names loses most of its force. Your name, Don Carlos, can very likely be yours on a label, registered, the way ten thousand Restrepos will never manage. So, there is your portfolio, the same as the other families, arranged in the opposite order. The method stays silent forever. The name goes loud."

Carlos was quiet for a moment, aligning the page with the edge of the table, and when he spoke, he was not really speaking to me.

"The same silence," he said. "Twenty-four years of the same silence. But now it has walls." He looked up. "In Valencia the silence was fear, Doctor. You are telling me that here, done correctly, it is an asset class."

"Done correctly," I said, "it is the oldest asset class your family owns."

Two families had stood at the same fork within ten days of each other and walked through opposite doors, both correctly, and both elections rested on the same quiet assumption that neither family had said aloud yet. Someone, soon, was going to have to manufacture these things at scale. A metered bottle does not come from a kitchen. A relaunch does not come from a garage. Somewhere north and west of that *panadería*, the factories were waiting with their quotes and their minimums and their smiling front offices, and I already knew, because it is my business to know, that there are exactly three kinds of men who run them.

CHAPTER NINE
The Three Factories

The kitchen hit its ceiling in the second week of October, when the salons asked for four hundred bottles and María, for the first time in nine years, had to say no to her own customers.

The arithmetic was not complicated. Two hundred bottles a month was the honest maximum of one woman, one daughter, one *comadre*, and two induction burners, and the metered bottle waiting inside its provisional application could not be filled by hand at all. Growth had stopped being a dream and become a logistics problem, and so we arrived at the sentence I had been saving since the first week.

"It is time to choose a factory," I told them, "and I want you to hear how this office thinks about that choice. You are not hiring a vendor. A vendor sells you boxes. A contract manufacturer stands inside your fence, holds pieces of what your family owns, and touches every bottle your customers will ever trust. You vet a partner like that the way you would vet a co-founder, because that is what he is, whether or not his name is on your company. And one more thing. I have arranged something, with permission from everyone involved, that I think you will thank me for. You are going to have company on these tours."

Carlos met us in the lobby on the morning of the first visit, in a guayabera pressed to architectural standards, and the two of them regarded each other for a moment with the curiosity of people who have heard of each other through walls.

"The lady of the amber bottle," Carlos said, with a small bow.

"The gentleman of the four pages," María said, and they shook hands like ambassadors, and neither of them asked me a single question about the other, because they both understood by then how my office worked. What Carlos brought was not information. It was eighteen years of standing inside production rooms, plus six more of delivering to loading docks across three counties, and a conviction, which I share, that a factory tells you the truth about itself in the first ten minutes if you know where to look.

"Doctor," he said in the elevator, "I will look at their floors and their scales and their people. You look at their papers. Between us, nobody will be able to lie."

* *

Romero & Sons had been filling bottles in Hialeah for thirty-four years, and walking into it was, for María, like walking into a memory she had never personally had.

Aurelio Romero met us at the door himself, seventy years old, in a shop coat with his name embroidered in script and gave us the tour of a man showing his house. The floors were clean. The machines were old and kept like violins. He knew every worker's name and most of their mothers, he pulled a warm bottle off the line to show us the fill level with genuine pride, and when María asked him what his contract looked like, he laughed and patted the air between them.

"Señora, my contract is thirty-four years of nobody complaining. Your word and mine. Ask anyone in Hialeah about Aurelio."

I watched María fall in love for the second time in this book. He was her mother's world, rebuilt in industrial form: trust as infrastructure, memory as filing system, the handshake as the only signature that counted. And I watched Carlos, five steps behind us, reading a different tour entirely. He paused at an open file room, unlocked, where batch sheets for a dozen client products sat in wire baskets an arm's length from the hallway. He watched a worker carry a clipboard from one client's line to another. And in the office, over *cafecito*, he asked Aurelio one gentle question, colleague to colleague.

"Don Aurelio, your people. How long do they stay?"

"Forever," Aurelio said warmly. "Well. Almost forever. My best mixer, Ramón, twelve years with me, went to a bigger shop up in Broward last spring. Good boy. He learned everything here." He said it the way you say a son graduated, with no shadow on his face at all, and I felt María's attention shift beside me, because she had spent a month building a fence, and she had just heard a man describe, with love, a gate standing open for twelve years.

In the car, she said it to herself before I could. "He is a good man. And his back office is my shoebox." She looked out the window at the shop as we pulled away. "Everything I was before you, *Licenciado*. Honest, careful, and open."

"Hold on to him anyway," I said. "Write his number in the book. An honest man with weak systems is a solvable problem, and before this is over, we may be very glad we know one."

* *

Meridian Formulation Group did not let us past the lobby until we had signed: a visitor confidentiality agreement, two pages, waiting on clipboards with our names already printed on them, before anyone had seen so much as a hallway. Camila read hers completely, out of new habit, and signed with something like appreciation. Carlos read his twice and looked, for the first time since I had met him, close to emotional.

The chief operating officer was a compact woman named Ingrid Vasallo, who ran the tour like a deposition she was winning, walking us past gowning stations, past segregated batch suites with electronic locks that logged every entry, past ingredient rooms where the labels faced out and the lot numbers marched in sequence. When Camila asked about employees, Ingrid answered before the question finished.

"Every person in this building signs confidentiality and non-use before they see a client hallway, and the ones who touch formulations sign more than that. We make visitors sign before we show them our corridors, señorita. Imagine what we make our chemists sign before we show them your family's file. Turnover is four percent. When someone does leave, we know what they know, because access is logged, and their exit interview includes a lawyer." She said it without warmth and without hostility, the way a wall states its height.

It was here that I raised the idea I had been carrying since the week of the fence, and I raised it as a question, to see what her face did.

"Suppose my client did not hand you the formula at all. Suppose one phase arrived at your dock already prepared, as a finished concentrate, made elsewhere, and your role was to compound the rest around it to a specification."

Ingrid's face did something I would describe, cautiously, as respect. "Then your client would be operating the way two of my largest accounts operate, and the way most of the small ones never think to. We would hold a recipe with a hole in the middle, and the hole would live wherever your client keeps it. It costs more. It is worth more." She looked at María with new attention. "Most people who walk in here want to hand me everything and hope. Yours wants to hand me a torso without a head. Who taught you that?"

"My mother," María said, which was true enough for a factory tour.

Then came the part of the visit where love meets arithmetic. Meridian's minimum run was five thousand units. Their fill cost, with the concentrate arrangement, came to two dollars and sixty cents a bottle against Romero's dollar seventy. The custom tooling for the two-chamber bottle, molds cut to the family's own design, would run twenty-two thousand dollars, and Ingrid quoted it without blinking and added one sentence that I made sure Camila wrote down. "The molds can be yours or ours depending on the contract. Clients who let us own the tooling save money in March and regret it for a decade."

In the parking lot, Camila did the full arithmetic out loud, and the total for a first run, molds and ingredients and labels and the concentrate equipment for María's own kitchen-side operation, landed a little north of forty thousand dollars, and María laughed once, without much joy, at a number she recognized.

"Forty thousand," she said. "The price of doing it correctly is the price Osvaldo offered me for all of it."

* *

Nu-Glo Laboratories quoted us a dollar fifteen a unit before we had told them what the product was.

The principal was a young man named Sammy who came around his desk to shake hands with both hands, called everyone by first name inside of a minute, and used the word *family* four times before we sat down. The tour was fast and gleaming in the front and got vague as it went back. Nu-Glo could start in three weeks. Nu-Glo did not need all those specifications; their chemists would figure it out. Nu-Glo's chemists could even improve the formula, no charge, they did it for clients all the time, and at that point I felt Carlos, beside me, go still the way hunting dogs go still.

Their agreement was one page. Sammy slid it across the desk with the smile of a man doing you a favor. "Standard," he said. "We keep it simple. Lawyers make everything so complicated, no offense, Ruben."

"None taken," I said, and read it, and it was a masterpiece, in the way traps are.

But the education of that afternoon did not come from the page. It came from the showroom, a proud wall of glass shelves by the exit where Nu-Glo displayed the brands it produced, and Camila, who misses nothing with a label on it, stopped walking in front of it. On the third shelf stood a serum bottle we all knew from a livestream, orange cap, flame on the label, FuegoGrow, hero product of a man with two hundred thousand followers. And beside it, in the same bottle, with the same cap, with the same fill line, stood a serum called VolcaniQ Growth Elixir, from a brand none of us had ever heard of, and the two of them sat there together like twins in different school uniforms.

"Same bottle," Camila said quietly.

"Same everything," Carlos said, not quietly at all, because he had stopped performing politeness somewhere around the ingredient room, where he had clocked a floor scale with a calibration sticker eleven months expired, mixing drums labeled in grease pencil, and one crew moving between two clients' lines without so much as a glove change. "Sammy. This VolcaniQ. Same formulation as the orange one?"

"Similar profile," Sammy said smoothly. "Lots of overlap in this category, you know how it is. Listen, before you go, one thing that helps us with logistics." He turned the smile on María. "You mentioned salons. If you leave us the list, the accounts, we can quote you delivery direct to—"

"No," Camila said, pleasantly, before her mother's hospitality could finish clearing its throat, "she didn't mention salons," which was true, because nobody had.

We debriefed in the car, in the parking lot, with the one-page agreement flat on my knee, and I gave them the autopsy line by line, because a trap you have dissected once is a trap you recognize forever.

"Confidentiality: Nu-Glo will exercise reasonable discretion with client information. That sentence promises nothing, defines nothing, and survives nothing. There is no non-use clause at all, meaning nothing on this page forbids them from taking what they learn from your file and making product with it, which, judging by the twins on that shelf, is not an oversight, it is the business model. Here, improvements: any enhancements or derivative formulations developed by Nu-Glo remain the property of Nu-Glo. Their free chemists are not a gift; they are a title transfer. No non-circumvention, and you heard him fish for the salon list with his own mouth, in the lobby, on the first date. Venue in their county, term of confidentiality two years, and after two years, señora, your grandmother's inheritance would belong to the reasonable discretion of Sammy." I folded the page once. "The cheapest quote in this industry is routinely the most expensive contract in it. A dollar fifteen is not their price. It is their bait, and the difference between bait and price is whatever your formula turns out to be worth to their other clients."

Carlos delivered the operational verdict, staring back at the building. "That is not a factory, Doctor. That is a fishing net with a loading dock." Then, quieter, with something old in his voice: "In Valencia, at the end, men like that circled everything that was still alive. They are always charming. They are always fast. And they are always cheapest, because the product they are actually buying walks in the front door and pays for the privilege."

María looked back at the glass showroom, at the shelf we could no longer see, and asked the question the whole day had been building. "The boy with the flames. Victor. He signed that page."

"Someone like him signs it every week," I said, which was as much as I could say, and more than I needed to, because Camila was already looking at her phone, at a video posted three days earlier, Victor grinning in a gleaming front hallway I had walked through personally that afternoon, captioned "day in the life at MY factory," and the algorithm, which respects no one's confidences, auto played him shaking hands with both hands with a man he called, four times, *family*.

* *

The choice, in the end, took the family eleven minutes, and the eleven minutes were not really about the factory.

"The fortress," María said. "Meridian. The woman with the walls." She said it looking at the numbers Camila had written, forty thousand dollars and change, the price of Osvaldo, the price of correctly. "We pay for the walls, and I keep the head of the recipe in my kitchen, and their people sign more than their visitors do. That is the fence, continued by other means." She exhaled. "How do we pay for it, *Licenciado*, I do not yet know, and I can see in your face that this is its own chapter."

"Two chapters," I said, "and the nearer one comes first, because choosing Meridian and being ready to sign Meridian are different countries. Their contract is forty-one pages. I have read it twice. There are eleven pages I like, twenty-two I can live with, and eight we are going to war about, starting with a minimum order that would eat this family's savings in one bite, a quality standard that does not yet say who decides what defective means, and a tooling clause that would make Ingrid's company the owner of a mold your family designed and paid for." I started the car. "So, before any ink, señora, we are going to do the thing that terrifies people more than signing does. We are going to negotiate, and at least once, I promise you now, we are going to stand up from that table and walk out the door, and walking will be the most valuable clause we get."

In the back seat, Carlos laughed, once, the laugh of a man who had sat on the other side of such tables for eighteen years and offered the only comfort available.

"Señora," he said, "the good ones respect you more when you leave. It is only the fishing nets that never let you reach the door."

CHAPTER TEN
Ink Before Batch

The rule of this office is three words long, and I made María and Camila repeat it back to me before we prepared for the hardest table of their year: ink before batch.

Nothing gets mixed, filled, labeled, or promised until the paper that governs it is signed, because a contract is not a formality that follows a deal. A contract is a machine for deciding future arguments in advance, and the only time you can build that machine honestly is before the first argument exists, while both sides are still courting and nobody has a defective pallet to blame on anybody. Somewhere across town, a young man had run five thousand units through a fishing net on the strength of one page and a group chat. We were going to do the opposite of everything he had done, in order, on purpose.

The preparation took two evenings, and the preparation was negotiation. Everything after it was theater with consequences.

"First," I told them, "we decide our no before we hear their yes. A negotiation is lost at the moment of maximum wanting, not at the table, and the only defense is a set of limits chosen in the calm. So, we will write them now. The most this family can commit against its bank balance. The terms we would rather delay launch than accept. And the signal." I capped my pen and set it down. "When I do that at their table, we thank everyone warmly and we stand up. No speeches, no anger, no door slamming. We simply leave, and señora, I promise you it will feel like dying, and it will be the most valuable clause we get."

"And second," Camila said, reading my outline upside down, which she had gotten good at, "we build the other table."

"We build the other table. Your power in any room is the door, and the door is only real if something is behind it. So, before we sit with the fortress, we are going to turn an honest man in Hialeah into a genuine alternative, on real paper, at a real price. Not as a bluff. As a plan we would happily live with. The classic bottle does not need custom molds or a metered fill. Romero can run two thousand units of it next month for a fraction of Meridian's minimum, and the concentrate solves his open back office, because a man cannot leak a head he has never held. If the fortress is not reasonable, the launch goes through Hialeah, the metered bottle waits for its moment, and nobody at this table ever negotiates from desperation again."

Camila ran the two futures side by side in her spreadsheet, and the numbers told the whole story of the month. Meridian's opening paper wanted five thousand units minimum, half the product cost as a deposit at signing, and the molds, all twenty-two thousand dollars of them, paid in full up front. The total commitment came to about forty-seven thousand dollars, and the total in the family's accounts, counting everything, came to thirty-four.

"So, their first offer is a company we cannot afford to be," Camila said.

"Their first offer is a form," I said. "Forms are written for the client who signs on the first date. We are going to introduce them to a different kind of client."

The limits page took most of the second evening. We wrote the ceiling on the signing check. We wrote the terms we would rather delay launch than accept. We wrote the signal, and María practiced not looking at me when I gave it.

I want that page to stay in your mind, because I am going to bring it back at the end of this chapter and show you what was missing from it.

* *

The negotiation at Meridian lasted four hours, and the first three went better than anyone deserved.

Ingrid Vasallo negotiated the way she toured, without decoration, with her contracts file open and her counsel on the speakerphone twice. Some of the eight pages I had marked for war surrendered before lunch. Ownership of improvements went to the family in one exchange, Ingrid signing off with a sentence I intend to keep. "We assign improvements to the client. We are not Nu-Glo, and I would rather lose an account than be confused with one." Non-circumvention went through, and so did the bar on subcontracting without written consent. Insurance followed, with the company named as an additional insured and the certificate attached, and venue in Miami-Dade with attorney fees to the prevailing party earned only a shrug and a yes. Confidentiality was rewritten to survive forever as to trade secrets, instead of expiring in two years like a certain single page we had all read in a parking lot. Even the molds moved: the family would pay for them, own them outright, and hold a written right to remove them within thirty days, and Meridian would charge a storage fee for the privilege, which is the fortress way of saying yes.

I want you to remember that storage fee too. Everybody at that table treated it as a rounding error, including me, and it was the only clause in the document that would eventually be triggered by our own victory.

The fight, when it came, came where fights live, which is in the definitions and the money.

"Conforming product," their form said, "means product meeting Meridian's standard tolerances," and I read that sentence out loud twice and then asked the room who would decide, eight months from now, whether a batch that smelled faintly wrong was defective. Because here is the argument I can see from years away: a pallet arrives, María opens a bottle, and it is not her mother's product, and Meridian's instruments say every number is inside tolerance. Whose nose wins? If the contract does not answer that question today, a judge answers it in three years, expensively, and the customer answers it first.

So we built the answer into the machine: a specification with numbers where numbers exist, viscosity, color, fill weight, ranges agreed in writing; a golden sample, one sealed reference bottle from the approved pilot batch, signed by both sides across the cap and kept in duplicate, one in each building, as the standard every future batch must match; an inspection window of ten business days after delivery, with written rejection rights and a remedy ladder, rework, then replace, then refund, in that order, chosen now; and, for the day the numbers pass and the nose still objects, a named third-party laboratory as tiebreaker, with the loser paying for the testing. Ingrid fought the nose hardest, because instruments are her religion, and she gave in only when I pointed out that the clause protected her too, since a client with a defined path to complain is a client with no excuse for an ambush.

Then the money, and the wall.

On the five thousand units, she would not move. It was not greed; she walked us through the setup economics of a custom-tooled, metered fill, the line time, the changeover cost, and the truth is her arithmetic was honest. And the deposit structure stood behind it, and Camila's spreadsheet sat between María and me with its two totals showing, forty-seven committed against thirty-four alive, and that is the moment I watched desperation arrive at the table wearing my client's face.

María had the pen in her hand. I had not seen her pick it up. "We are so close," she said quietly, to me, in Spanish, the words themselves leaning forward. "The bottles are real, the name is real, the fence is built, everything is finally..." She stopped herself. "I can find the difference. The salons would advance me something. Or..." And she did not say the name, but I watched it cross her mind, the distributor with the checkbook and the patience, the man who still bought two cases a month as if nothing had happened, and who would like nothing better than to become this company's necessary friend.

"Señora," I said, "put down the pen and look at the limits we wrote on Tuesday." She looked. The number on the page was the number we had chosen in the calm, and the number on the table was bigger, and between those two numbers is where companies sign the mistakes that take years to unwind. Money borrowed in the moment of maximum wanting is the most expensive money in the world, and money borrowed from a man who once tried to buy you is not money at all. It is a leash with interest. I capped my pen and set it down on the table.

We stood. We thanked them, warmly and honestly, because everything they had agreed to was real and everything they had refused had a reason. Ingrid walked us to the elevator herself, unoffended, reading the situation with professional appreciation, and what she said as the doors opened was almost exactly what a truck driver had prophesied from the back seat.

"Most people sign on the first date," she said. "Go price your alternative, Mr. Alcoba. This paper does not expire, and neither do I."

The elevator doors closed, and María let out a breath she had been holding for approximately four hours, and Camila said, to the ceiling, "That felt like dying."

"I promised it would," I said. "Now we are going make the door real."

* *

Aurelio Romero read the agreement I had drafted for him the way a man reads a letter from an old country, holding it slightly away from himself, and for a long moment I thought we had lost him.

"Thirty-four years," he said. "Nobody has ever handed me one of these. My word and their word. That has been the whole machinery, mi socio." He set the pages down on his desk, next to a photograph of the shop in 1991. "And now the lady with the beautiful product wants Aurelio to sign like a stranger."

It was his son who turned it, which I had half expected, because the son had been standing in the doorway with his arms crossed and the expression of a man watching a bus he had been waiting five years for finally arrive. Ernesto Romero, called Neto, ran the shop's operations now, and he crossed the room, picked up the agreement, and read it standing, fast, the way Camila read things.

"Papi. Look at what it actually says." He turned the pages toward his father one at a time. "It says her secret comes in as a prepared concentrate, so this shop never holds the whole recipe. That is not an insult, which is a client protecting us from ever being blamed for a leak we could not have caused. It says defective gets defined by a sealed sample and numbers, in writing, so the day a batch is wrong, we are not arguing about anybody's nose. It says who pays if something goes badly, and it names a court in this county, and it makes them keep our confidences the same as we keep theirs." He set the pages down. "Papi, I have been asking you for paper like this for five years. Ramón walked out of here with twelve years of clients' processes in his head and we could do nothing, and you called it graduation. This is the first client who has ever respected the shop enough to protect it from itself."

Aurelio looked at his son for a moment, and then at me, and something in his face reorganized itself around a truth arriving late but intact.

"The concentrate," he said slowly. "She keeps the head. I fill the body. And if anything ever walks out my door in somebody's memory, it cannot be the part that matters." He picked up the pen. "You know, mi socio, my father filled bottles in Regla before the revolution, on a handshake, and the handshake worked because everyone would know everyone for fifty years. Here, people graduate." He signed both copies in a careful old hand. "Two thousand units of the classic. Tell the señora her secret is safe in Hialeah and tell her it is safe because she never sent it."

* *

We went back to Meridian eleven days later, and the table had changed shape, because we had changed it.

I will compress the wins, because leverage is boring to watch and beautiful to own. The family no longer needed Meridian to launch. Two thousand classic bottles were already scheduled through Hialeah on signed paper at a price the bank balance could laugh at, which meant the metered bottle, the crown of the line, could arrive when the terms deserved it, and Ingrid, to her lasting credit, understood the new geometry in about ninety seconds and negotiated like a woman relieved to finally be dealing with an adult. The five thousand units survived, because her setup arithmetic was real, but the structure of them bent: one commitment, two releases, twenty-five hundred now and twenty-five hundred within nine months, with the deposit restructured to follow the releases. The signing check fell from thirty-one thousand dollars to fourteen. The molds stayed family owned. The golden sample, the inspection window, the remedy ladder, the laboratory tiebreaker, all of it rode into the final draft untouched, and page by page, the form Meridian offered to every first-date client became the machine this family would live inside.

That is where I would have ended this chapter a few years ago, and I want you to notice how good it sounds, and how it is not the whole page.

Because when the structure of the run bent, the price of the run moved, and Ingrid did not hide it, and she did not apologize for it either. She turned to the fill schedule with a pen, the way a person turns to arithmetic they have already done in their head.

"Two releases are two setups," she said. "Changeover on a custom tool, line time twice, and a fresh QC validation on the second release because nine months is long enough that I will not certify the first one's readings. That is thirty-eight cents a bottle. Your fill goes from two sixty to two ninety-eight."

Camila found the number on her screen before I did. She did not say anything. She looked at me, once, and I have thought about that look a great deal since.

"For clarity," Ingrid went on, "you did not negotiate a discount, Mr. Alcoba. You negotiated a schedule, and schedules are financed. The finance charge lives in the fill price. It is the same money in a different currency, and in your position, I would have made the same trade, which is why I am not going to insult you by pretending it is a favor."

And then, because she was thorough and because it is her building, she turned two pages back to the clause I had won in the first session, the one everyone had treated as a rounding error.

"Your molds are yours. They will also sit on my floor for nine months between releases, doing nothing, in a space I could rent to a client running product. The storage fee is a hundred and fifty a month. That is your clause, negotiated by you, and I am invoking it exactly as written."

I had drafted that clause. I was pleased with that clause. I had considered it a small trophy, and it was, and the trophy had a subscription attached, and I had not seen it because on the day I won it there had been only one release and the molds were never going to sit idle.

We signed. It was the right agreement, and I would sign it again. But I had come into that room believing I had bought something for nothing, and I left it having bought something on credit, and the difference between those two sentences is a lesson I paid for in front of my own client.

* *

The signing had one piece of ceremony in it, and I confess I staged it, because some clauses deserve a photograph. On the conference table between María and Ingrid stood the pilot bottle, the approved reference, the standard against which every future batch would be judged, and the two women signed their names across the seal of its cap, one signature from each building, ink meeting glass.

"A future argument," Ingrid said, examining the result, "already decided."

"That is the entire technology," I said.

María held the sealed bottle up to the window light the way she had once held a label mockup, at arm's length, then close. "My mother settled arguments by being right forty years," she said. "This is faster."

* *

Camila came to the office alone the next morning, which she had never done, and she came with the spreadsheet already open.

"I need to show you something and I need you to not manage me through it," she said. "I ran it last night instead of sleeping."

She turned the laptop around. She had built two columns.

"Column one. What walking away saved us. The signing check went from thirty-one thousand to fourteen. Seventeen thousand dollars. That is real and it happened once and it is the reason this company still exists in November, so nobody is taking that away from you."

"Column two."

"Column two is thirty-eight cents." She scrolled. "Thirty-eight cents on every bottle Meridian ever fills for us. Not on the first five thousand. On the tier. That price is now our price, and every renewal quote in that building starts from two ninety-eight instead of two sixty, forever, unless we get big enough to renegotiate it, and getting big enough is the plan, so the number is going to ride with us the entire way up." She stopped scrolling and let the cursor sit on one cell. "Seventeen thousand divided by thirty-eight cents is forty-four thousand seven hundred and thirty-seven bottles. That is the crossover. Bottle number forty-four thousand seven hundred and thirty-eight is the one where the thing we won turns into the thing we paid."

"And when do we get there."

"Month twenty-two." She closed the laptop halfway, which for Camila is a gesture of mourning. "On our own projections. On the projections we made because we believe them."

I want to write down exactly what I did next, because it was the correct thing and I did not do it gracefully.

I did not tell her she was wrong. She was not wrong; her arithmetic was better than mine and she had done it on her own time because it frightened her. I did not tell her it was the cost of doing business, which is the phrase men use when they would rather not name a number. What I did was go to the drawer, take out the limits page from the second evening, put it on the table between us, and read it out loud.

Every line on that page was denominated in the same thing. The ceiling on the signing check. The cash the family could commit. The most we would pay at the moment of signing. I had spent two evenings teaching a family to defend itself, and every wall I built ran along one axis, and the axis I chose was the one that frightened my client in the room she was sitting in.

There was no line on that page about cost per unit over time. There was no line about what a concession does to a tier. There was no line reading *what will this be worth in month twenty-two*, because in the calm of a Tuesday evening in an office, with a woman across from me who had nearly signed away three generations for forty thousand dollars, the danger I could see was the danger of a check she could not write, and I defended her against it completely and against nothing else.

"So, it was a mistake," Camila said.

"No. It was a trade, and I made it half blind. Those are different failures and the second one is mine." I turned the page over and wrote on the back of it, in front of her, because a lesson that stays in a lawyer's head is a lesson the client paid for and did not receive. "Here is what goes on every limits page this office ever writes again. One. The most we will pay at signing. Two. The most we will pay per unit, over time, at the volumes we actually intend to reach. And three, the one nobody writes, which is which of those two numbers we are choosing to lose, and why, in our own words, before we lose it."

"And what's our why?"

"That a company that cannot survive to month nine has no month twenty-two to argue about." I put the pen down. "Seventeen thousand dollars in November bought your mother the right to not borrow from Osvaldo. There is no version of the good outcome where she borrows from Osvaldo. So, we paid thirty-eight cents a bottle for the distance between this family and that man, and it was expensive, and it was correct, and the reason I am not going to tell you it was free is that in month twenty-two you are going to open this spreadsheet again and I want you to find that I already knew."

Camila looked at the page for a while.

"You wrote it on the back," she said.

"I did."

"Not the front."

"The front is what we knew in the calm," I said. "The back is what it cost to find out."

* *

The golden sample's twin came home to my office, and Alexa found it on the shelf that afternoon, next to the amber bottles, the named one and the nameless one, a small museum accumulating on the corner of my desk.

"There's writing on the cap," she said, tilting it. "Two signatures. What is it, evidence?"

"The opposite," I said. "Evidence is what you collect after the fight. That is a fight that will never need to happen, sealed in advance. Ink before batch."

She set it back with unusual care. Then she nodded at the limits page, which was still on my desk, turned over.

"Is that the thing you've been reading since ten o'clock?"

"It is."

"Front or back?"

I have never been entirely sure how much that girl assembled from the lobby, and I stopped asking somewhere around this week.

"Back," I said.

"Good," she said, and went to answer the phone.

I would have ended the week there, in the quiet after good paper, except that companies do not pause to admire their own machinery. Two thousand bottles were now scheduled to exist in five weeks, and bottles that exist require labels that exist, real ones, printed and die-cut and glued, not trimmed with scissors at two in the morning, and Camila had already told her mother the truth every founder with a laptop eventually tells: production art was past the edge of what she could do alone. So, the calls had gone out through the family's usual switchboard, which is to say through Reina, and Reina knew someone, an artist, gifted, half the price of the agencies, practically family.

I have been a lawyer in this community for twenty years. Nothing in it has ever cost my clients more than the phrase practically family, and the artist was coming on Tuesday.

PART IV
THE BRAND AND THE LINE

CHAPTER ELEVEN
The Face on the Label

They did not bring me the artist. They brought me the art, ten days after the artist had finished it, and by then everyone had already cried, and the invoice had already been paid.

María laid the printed proofs on my conference table the way relics get laid on altars, and I will not pretend the room stayed professional, because the work was extraordinary. The front label held everything the family had decided in the naming chapter of their lives, the amber field, the thin strip rendered like masking tape, AMBARINA in Marta's reconstructed hand. And above the name, where a lesser designer would have put a flourish, there was a portrait. It was Marta herself, in soft gouache, painted from the photograph on María's refrigerator, the one with the stricter mouth and María's eyes, except the artist had found something in the face that the photograph had only implied, a patience, a competence, the look of a woman mid-thought about somebody else's problem. On the back panel, in small, justified type, ran the story Camila had written, three generations, a wood stove in Antioquia, a folding table at a church in Miami, and the sentence ended with her name, Marta, 1941 to 2019, *siempre presente.*

"Her name was Paloma," Camila said. "Reina's neighbor's daughter. Art school, works retail, freelances nights. Profe, she took the refrigerator photo home on a Sunday and came back the next Sunday with Abuela's face. Mamá cried. I cried. Luz cried and Luz didn't even like the first draft of the tape stripe." She smoothed the proof with one finger. "Nine hundred dollars. The agencies quoted six thousand and a mood board. She did it for nine hundred because we're practically family."

I let the proofs have their silence, because they had earned it, and then I asked the question my job requires me to ask at the exact moment nobody wants to hear it.

"It is beautiful. It may be the single most valuable thing this company has commissioned. Now show me the agreement."

The silence changed temperature. María and Camila looked at each other, and in that look, I watched ten chapters of discipline meet the one word that had beaten it. "It was a label, *Licenciado*," María said. "Not a contract. She is Reina's neighbor. She gave us a gift price. You do not hand a contract to someone who has just given you back your mother's face."

"Señora," I said, as gently as the sentence allows, "then let me tell you what you bought for nine hundred dollars, and what you did not. Under the law of this country, the person who creates a work of art owns it at the moment of creation. Automatically, with no filing and no discussion, the way your formula belonged to your family the moment your grandmother composed it. Paying for the work buys you the work, the object, the files she delivered. It does not buy the copyright, unless a signed writing says so, and no writing exists. So here is the estate of things this morning. Paloma owns your mother's portrait. Paloma owns the label design. This family owns some very beautiful printouts and the right, almost certainly, to use them as intended, because a designer paid to make a label has at least impliedly permitted the label. But permission is not a possession. You bought a painting, and she kept the printing press, and a label, señora, is nothing in this world but copies."

Camila had gone through her phone to the invoice, as if the invoice might contain a clause nobody remembered. "But work for hire," she said. "That's a thing. I've literally seen it on freelance sites. If you pay someone to make something, it's work for hire and the company owns it."

"It is a thing, and it is the most misunderstood thing in this field, so learn it properly once. Work made for hire has two doors. The first is for true employees creating within their jobs, and Paloma is nobody's employee. The second is for specially commissioned works, and it requires a signed writing, and even then, the law only honors it for certain listed categories, and a product label fits those categories awkwardly at best. Which is why, in this office, we do not gamble on magic words. The words that move a copyright are not work for hire. They are hereby assigns, in writing, signed by the artist. Belt and suspenders, and we are currently wearing neither."

"Okay," Camila said slowly, "but functionally, today, what can go wrong? She loves us. The label prints, we launch, who is harmed?"

The universe, which enjoys my job more than I do, answered her before I could. María's phone rang, and it was Reina, and María listened for a moment and then put her hand flat on the table the way she does when the floor moves. Paloma, honorable to the bone, had called Reina to ask a courtesy question. She was assembling her professional portfolio, finally, at a friend's urging. Could she include the Ambarina label? Because she had posted one corner of the portrait online, just the eyes, just to test the response, and a skincare startup out of Orlando had already messaged her asking who owned the style and whether she was available to do *a grandmother label like that one* for them.

"She was asking permission," María said, lowering the phone. "She owns my mother's face, and she was asking us for permission."

"Which tells you everything about her character," I said, "and nothing about your position. Character is not a chain of title. Tuesday, we fix the paper."

* *

Paloma came on Tuesday, and she was not what the word freelancer had led anyone to expect, because nobody expects the quiet ones to be the dangerous ones.

She was twenty-seven, carried a portfolio case older than she was, and sat with her hands folded while I said what I am required to say to an unrepresented person on the other side of a deal. I was the company's lawyer, not hers. Nothing I said today was advice to her. She was free, and encouraged, to have anyone she trusted review whatever we proposed. She nodded and said she already had a friend from art school who did contracts for illustrators now, and the friend had explained to her, for the first time in her life, what she had been giving away at friend prices for nine years.

"So, I have a number," she said, and then she did the thing that made María's breath change. She apologized for it. "It is more than before. I am sorry. I know it was supposed to be a favor, and Reina will be embarrassed, and I don't want anyone to think that I..." She made herself stop. She took the folded page from her portfolio and set it on the table and pressed it flat, the way another woman in this book once pressed a strip of masking tape into a notebook. "Four thousand. For everything. The assignment, the exclusivity, all rights, forever. My friend says I should ask for more. But you were the first clients who treated my work like it was worth stealing, so." She folded her hands again. "Four thousand. I am sorry."

The room held still, and I watched María look at this girl, twenty-seven years old, apologizing for the value of her own inheritance, and I watched nine months of this family's education arrive on María's face all at once.

"*Mija*," María said quietly. "Nine months ago, a man offered me forty thousand dollars for everything my mother ever made, and I came to this office to ask if the paper was legal, because I did not believe I was allowed to ask any other question. I sat where you are sitting. I apologized the way you are apologizing." She reached across and turned Paloma's page right side up, facing the girl, not us. "Do not ever say sorry for the price again. Not to us, not to anyone. You are not expensive, *mija*. You were cheap for nine years, and that is a different sentence." She looked at me. "Pay her."

We built the agreement that afternoon, and I built it the way I wish someone had built things for a hundred artists I have watched get skinned in this town. The company received a full assignment, hereby assigns, in writing, signed, of the portrait, the label, and every file, with the copyright to be registered in the company's name, because registration is the courthouse key, the thing that turns ownership into enforcement. Paloma received her four thousand dollars, and she also received what the standard forms never think to give: the permanent right to show the work in her portfolio, with credit, as hers in authorship forever even though ours in ownership, and a restraint she suggested herself before I could draft it, that she would not create confusingly similar grandmother-portrait labels for competing hair and beauty brands. The Orlando startup received a polite no. And the file received one more page, the template that would govern every pixel, photograph, jingle, and line of code this company ever commissioned again, so that no future contributor would ever be anything but one of two things, an owner or an assignor, with the difference in writing.

When it was signed, Camila did the arithmetic out loud, because that is her love language. "Four thousand now, minus the nine hundred then. We paid three thousand one hundred dollars for a missing sentence."

"You paid three thousand one hundred dollars," I said, "to learn, before launch, with a kind counterparty, at friend prices, a lesson that companies routinely learn years later, from a stranger, in front of a judge, with the whole brand held hostage. There are law schools that charge more per credit. This was the cheapest tuition this company will ever pay, and I want it remembered exactly this way: art was never the risk. The gratitude was. You were all so busy being grateful that nobody asked who owned the thing you were grateful for."

María gathered the signed pages, and she said the sentence I have been quoting to clients ever since. "So that is the rule for love and business together. The favor and the paper are not enemies. The favor is why the paper is generous. The paper is why the favor cannot be regretted."

* *

Doña Rosa came on Thursday, sent by Juliana, which is how I learned that my clients had begun to find each other in the wild, trading my office's name across salon chairs like a remedy.

She was somewhere past sixty and carried herself like hospitality itself, and she ran a salon in Coral Gables that I had heard of the way one hears of restaurants without menus. She had run it for twenty-two years, for a clientele she would not name and did not need to, because half of them had been photographed leaving her chairs by people who make a living photographing car doors. She sat down, refused coffee twice before accepting it, which is the proper form, and told me she had come because of a label.

"Juliana showed me a picture of it. The bottle with the grandmother." She touched her own chest. "*Con permiso*, I did not sleep after. Because I thought that family put their inheritance on a piece of paper and now, they own it. And I have twenty-two years, *Licenciado*. I have the best chairs in this city. Women fly in. And this week I asked myself for the first time, what do I own?" She counted on her fingers, gently, like someone counting an absence. "The name of my salon, I never registered it. The sign? A client's nephew painted it in 2009. A lovely boy. We paid him in haircuts. The famous ones post my mirror, my hands, my little logo. Millions of people see it, and none of that is on any paper anywhere. I always said that my brand is my hands." She looked at her hands, then at me, with the smallest smile I had seen in that office all year. "You cannot register hands."

"No, señora," I said. "But everything your hands have built for twenty-two years is sitting in a pile, unclaimed, and you are the only person with the right to claim it, for now. So, we will start where everyone starts." I reached for the legal pad, and she laughed before I finished the motion, because Juliana had warned her.

"The four pages," she said. "I brought a pen."

* *

That evening, alone in the office, I did the last thing on the label file, which was to read it, not admire it, the way the government reads, one claim at a time.

The front was clean. The name promised nothing, which was the entire genius of the name. But the back panel, the beautiful back panel, Camila's three generations in small, justified type, contained a sentence I must have let my eyes slide across four times while they were wet: *For seventy years, the women of one family have trusted this formula for stronger, fuller, healthier hair.*

There they were, stronger, fuller, healthier, three words resting quietly inside a love letter, each one a doorbell at a different regulator's house, and on Monday I was going to have to walk two proud women through the difference between what their customers may swear and what their label may say. I pinned the proof to the corkboard behind my desk, and beside it I pinned something I had been saving for exactly this occasion, printed from a public database that afternoon: a warning letter, from the federal government to a hair-serum company I will not name here, itemizing sentences, quoting a label back to its owner the way prosecutors quote diaries.

Two documents hung side by side on a corkboard now: the most beautiful label I had ever been handed, and the anatomy of what happens to beautiful labels that say one word too many.

CHAPTER TWELVE
The Line Between a Bottle and a Drug

I opened the hardest meeting of the family's regulatory life by reading them somebody else's mail.

María and Camila sat at my conference table under the corkboard, where the most beautiful label I had ever been handed hung beside a letter from the federal government to a hair-serum company neither of them had heard of, and before we touched a word of their own copy, I read the letter out loud, not all of it, only the parts that mattered.

"Listen to how it begins. The government reviewed the company's product labels, its website, and its social media accounts. Then listen to what it quotes. Not the ingredient panel. The captions. Stimulates dormant follicles. Clinically proven regrowth. Watched your edges come back, thanks to us. The letter takes the company's own Instagram posts and reads them back like a diary in a courtroom, and then it delivers the sentence this entire meeting exists to prevent. Because of these claims, the letter says, your products are drugs. Not because of what is in the bottle. Nobody tested the bottle. Because of what the company said about the bottle. And unapproved drugs may not be sold in this country, which converts every unit in their warehouse, by operation of their own marketing, into contraband."

María was looking at the letter the way people look at accident footage. "Who are they?"

"Nobody in particular, señora, which is the point. A small company. Ambitious. Probably sincere. Almost certainly a company whose customers really did swear the product worked, and who made the one mistake this family is here today to refuse. They believed their customers out loud, on the label, in the seller's own voice."

"So today," Camila said, eyeing the beautiful proof beside the letter, "you operate on Abuela."

"Today we learn the line, because everything about your next ten years depends on which side of it this family speaks from. The law divides everything in a bottle into two kingdoms, and the border is not chemistry.

It is intention, and intention is proven by words. A cosmetic is a product intended to cleanse, beautify, promote attractiveness, and alter appearance. A drug is a product intended to affect the structure or function of the body, or to treat or prevent disease. Same bottle, same formula, same grandmother. If the label says softens and smooths, the bottle is a cosmetic. If the label says regrows, the bottle is a drug, unapproved, illegal to ship, and the government does not need a laboratory to prove it. It needs a screenshot. Your words are the product, legally speaking. The name can be a claim. The caption can be a claim. A customer's testimonial becomes your claim the moment you repeat it in the seller's voice. So." I took down the proof and laid it between them, and I put my pen on the back panel, on the sentence I had found the night everyone else was crying. "Stronger. Fuller. Healthier. Word by word."

The surgery took an hour, and I will record it the way it happened, because the craft is the lesson.

"Stronger has a lawful life, if it wears its harness. Hair, the fiber itself, is not living tissue, and the whole industry lawfully speaks about how hair looks and feels. For hair that looks and feels stronger walks the cosmetic lane. Stronger hair, naked, begins to gesture at biology, and this family does not gesture at biology. Fuller is more dangerous, because fuller has a twin brother named more hair, and more hair means growth, and growth means follicles, and follicles are the body. The volumizing shelf survives on one hedge, and you will use it: the look of fuller hair. And healthier, señora, is the trickiest of the three, because it sounds the gentlest. Health is the body's word. Healthy-looking is the shelf's word, and the difference between those two is the difference between a label and an exhibit."

Camila had been holding it in for forty minutes, and it came out the way I expected, which is to say it honestly.

"This is where I fight you, Tío. Looks stronger. The look of fuller. Healthy-looking. Do you hear it? That's the grammar of liars. That's what the bad products say, the ones that don't work, weasel words, and ours *works*. Doña Carmen sat in a folding chair and cried telling me what it did. Seventeen women, and not one of them said my hair looked anything. They said grew. They said came back. The one completely true sentence about this product is the one sentence you're forbidding, and the mealy sentence you're prescribing is beneath it. We would be lying by under-telling the truth."

I let her finish, because the argument deserved its whole shape. It is the oldest temptation in this industry, and it does not feel like temptation. It feels like honesty. The lie that ruins companies is almost never invented in a marketing meeting. It is transcribed, faithfully, from a weeping customer, and it is true, and none of that matters, and I told her why in the language she respects most.

"Every claim has a price tag, Camila. Not a moral one. A literal one. The moment this family says grows in the seller's voice, it has entered the drug kingdom, and the drug kingdom has an admission fee. Studies. Clinical evidence of the kind that costs more than this company's first three years of revenue, conducted before you speak, reviewed by people in Maryland, for the right to sell a fourteen-dollar bottle at what would then have to be a ninety-dollar price in a lane this family cannot fund, staffed by professionals it cannot hire. That is not the government being cruel. That is the price of promising medicine, and it is the same for everyone, and it is why the shelf talks the way it talks. The companies saying healthy-looking are not all liars, *mija*. Some of them are people who did the arithmetic. And now hear the strategy underneath the restraint, because your family is holding a better hand than you think. The label does not need to say grows. Doña Carmen says grows. Seventeen women say grows, at church, in salons, on the telephone to Barranquilla, for free, forever, in the one voice the law does not charge admission for, the customer's own. Your market was built by testimony, and it will grow by testimony. The seller stays silent about growth and the choir sings, and the company that has that choir and still insists on singing the solo itself is not brave. It is uninsurable."

Camila looked at the proof for a long moment. And then she did the thing she does, which is find the better answer inside the constraint.

"Then we split it," she said slowly. "The problem is that the story and the claim are fused in one sentence, so the claim poisons the story. Unfuse them. The back panel keeps the story, and the story makes no promises at all. For seventy years, the women of one family have trusted this formula. Period. That sentence is history. It's true, clean, and stronger without the adjectives, because trust for seventy years implies everything, we're not allowed to say. Then the front, tiny, under the name, carries the harnessed claim and nothing else. For the look and feel of stronger, fuller hair." She looked up. "The love letter stays a love letter. The claim goes in the claim's cage."

"Write it exactly that way," I said, "and understand what you just invented, because it is the whole discipline in one label. The story does the wanting. The claim does the promise. Never let one do the other's job."

María, who had said almost nothing through the surgery, touched the corner of the proof where the painted tape stripe ran under her mother's rebuilt handwriting. "And the old word," she said. "Fortalecedor. It stays in the museum?"

"It stays in the museum, señora. On the notebook, on your desk, in the story you tell reporters someday. Not on the pack. A descriptive word in Spanish translates into a claim in English, and we do not smuggle claims in a second language past a government that employs translators."

* *

Then came the part nobody warns families about, which is that the safe lane has homework too.

Choosing the cosmetic kingdom is not an exemption from law. It is an enrollment in a different one, newer and stricter than the one María's competitors grew up ignoring, and we spent the afternoon building the file. The manufacturing facilities had to be registered with the government, which Meridian was, certificate in the folder, and the product itself had to be listed, which became Camila's task, with its formula information handled through channels that did not require undressing the secret. The law now requires a safety file, adequate substantiation that the product is safe, and I watched Camila open a binder and begin assembling it, ingredient by ingredient, safety profile by safety profile, with the seventy-year history of use noted for what it honestly is, supporting evidence, not a substitute for the science. The label gained a line the family had never imagined, a company address through which any customer could report a harm, because the law now requires the seller to receive, record, and, for serious cases, report the bad news, and a company that sells to grandmothers, I told them, should want that mailbox even where the law forgot to require it.

And the label gained one more thing, and this one cost María visibly: the ingredient declaration, every component listed by its international name, in descending order, printed on the pack for the world to read, as the law requires of everyone.

She read the draft list twice, and I watched three generations of instinct fight one column of type. "The nouns," she finally said, remembering the word from the week the fence was built. "The shelf betrays the nouns."

"And keeps the verbs," I said. "The amounts, the order, the waiting, the source. Everything on that list, a competitor could learn in a laboratory next month anyway. You are not surrendering the secret, señora. You are paying the toll every lawful bottle pays, and the toll was priced into the fence from the first day."

She initialed the list in her mother's blue ballpoint, in the manner of a woman signing a treaty she had already won.

* *

Juliana arrived on Thursday with relaunch cards, and the relaunch cards said FORMALDEHYDE-FREE in gold foil, and by Friday they said nothing at all, because I had them in my drawer.

She had become proud, and she had every right; the four pages were done, the fence was rising, the new generation of her method was documented and walled. The cards were the last piece, GENTLE, NATURAL, FORMALDEHYDE-FREE, and I asked her one question that I ask every smoothing client, which is to show me the safety data sheet for her working solution, the manufacturer's own document, not the brochure. She had both. The brochure, glossy, said *advanced formaldehyde-free technology*. The safety sheet, in the fine columns nobody reads, listed an ingredient that releases formaldehyde when heated, and Juliana's entire method, like every method in her category, ends with a very hot iron.

I watched her read the two documents side by side, the brochure and the confession, and I watched a woman who had once given away her ratios to eighty thousand strangers understand that she had nearly done something worse, which is retail somebody else's lie in her own voice.

"They wrote *free*," she said quietly. "In their brochure. I believed the brochure, *meu Deus*, everyone believes the brochure. If I print their word on my card—"

"Then at the salon door their word becomes your word, and your word is the only one the law reads, and the letter on my corkboard gets a cousin with your name on it. Your supplier's marketing is not a shield, Juliana. It is a debt you inherit at retail. So, the claim freezes today. All three words because gentle and natural are promises too, and promises need files behind them, and building your file honestly is next month's work, yours and mine. It may end in reformulation. It may end in truthful, harder-won words that no competitor in your category can match, precisely because they are true. Either way, nothing gold-foiled leaves this office ahead of its evidence."

Juliana looked at the cards in my drawer for a moment. Then she pushed the drawer shut herself.

"Eighty thousand people watched me be generous once," she said. "They will not watch me be false. Print nothing, *querida*. I will wait for the words I can keep."

* *

Victor did not wait, because waiting was the one product Victor never carried.

Alexa gave me the update Friday evening, phone flat on the desk, with the dispassion of a coroner. Day thirty had arrived, as day thirty does, for the first five thousand customers of a serum whose label promised regrowth in exactly that many days or your money back, and the comment sections had turned into an accounting department: refund demands, side-by-side photos, one man holding a tape measure to his hairline with the caption "day 31, where is it." And Victor had answered the ledger the only way he knew, with a restock: FuegoGrow MAX, new label, the old promise plus a new gold burst that said LAB TESTED.

"Tested by what lab?" I asked.

"I looked," Alexa said. "There's a certificate in his video. He holds it up for one second. The letterhead is the factory's." She let that sit between us, next to the golden sample and the amber bottles, the desk museum where this family kept its decided arguments. "So that's the week. Two hair products went to print. One label got rewritten by a lawyer until every word could survive a screenshot. The other one doubled its promise and had its evidence printed by the man selling its twin under a different name." She pocketed the phone. "You keep telling me the law draws lines where they protect most people. Tell me the truth. Does anything happen to him?"

"Something is already happening to him," I said. "It is still in the mail."

I pinned the family's finished label to the corkboard that night, beside the warning letter, stood back and looked at the two of them together, and they no longer read as beauty and doom. They read as the two-lane markers of the same road, the sentence that survives and the sentences that testify, and between them, invisible, ran the line this chapter is named for. On Monday, Camila was bringing me the launch marketing plan, and I already knew from her calendar invitation what was at the top of it, because she had titled the file with the innocence of a person who has learned nine lessons and not yet the tenth: DOÑA CARMEN TELLS HER STORY, ON CAMERA.

The choir was free. The question waiting for Monday was what happens when the seller hands the choir a microphone.

CHAPTER THIRTEEN
What You May Say, and Who Must Say It Honestly

Camila kept her rule. I want that on the record before anything else in this chapter, because what went wrong that week went wrong around her, through the two channels no compliance plan ever thinks to cover: an aunt with a phone, and a mother discovering what it feels like to be liked.

The Monday meeting began correctly. Camila walked me through the launch plan slide by slide, nothing public until it went past me, exactly as she had promised in the week of the deleted teaser, and the plan was good, and we were halfway through the Doña Carmen video proposal when María's phone lit up on the table for the fourth time in ten minutes, and Camila glanced at the screen, and then looked at her mother the way auditors look at a second set of books.

"Mamá. Why is Reina's post in your notifications?"

What surfaced over the next twenty minutes was a campaign that no one had approved because no one had understood it to be a campaign. Reina, bursting with family pride, had posted the label, the portrait, and three paragraphs about her cousin's miracle formula, without a word anywhere about being the cousin. The sister in Queens, a reseller building her own market, had paid a local beauty creator two hundred and fifty dollars and a case of product to make a glowing video, and the video said everything except that anything had been paid. And María, the woman who once apologized for a bottle, had spent two weeks resharing all of it to her community status, with her own captions, including Doña Carmen's church testimony and a before-and-after photo that Camila enlarged, studied, and pronounced, in the flat voice of a forensic accountant, "shot at golden hour with a ring light."

María's confession, when it came, was so human it hurt to watch. "Four hundred views, *Licenciado*." She turned the phone around as if presenting evidence in her own defense and her own prosecution at once. "My status. Four hundred. I checked it at two in the morning. Me, checking numbers in the dark like a teenager, and every time somebody wrote *qué maravilla* under my mother's face, it felt like..." She stopped and put the phone face down. "It felt like being paid for something I did not know I was hungry for."

"Then let me tell you what the law calls what happened," I said, "because none of it requires anyone at this table to have been dishonest, which is exactly what makes it dangerous. The rules on advertising are built on one idea. A recommendation is worth more when it looks free, so the law requires the price tag to show. Anyone speaking about a product must disclose what connects them to it, if the connection would matter to the person listening. Money is a connection. Free product is a connection. And family, señora, is a connection, the oldest one there is. Reina's three paragraphs are beautiful, and they are also, in the eyes of the rules, an undisclosed endorsement by the seller's own cousin. The video from Queens is a paid advertisement wearing the costume of an opinion. And your statuses." I turned to her gently, because this part was going to cost her the most. "Every time the brand's owner reshares a customer saying it made her hair grow back, the law hears the seller saying it. You adopted the choir, señora. In writing. With captions. The microphone we spent all last week not handing out, the family handed out three ways without noticing, because in your world this is not advertising. It is telling people good news. The law does not have a category for good news."

* *

The letter arrived Thursday, which told me someone had been watching the statuses as closely as María had.

It came from a downtown firm on behalf of a client identified as NR Beauty Distribution LLC, and it was polite artillery of a familiar caliber: the reshared testimonials characterized as false and unsubstantiated advertising, the ring-light photograph as a deceptive demonstration, the undisclosed family and paid endorsements itemized with screenshots, a demand to cease, to preserve, to correct. Two of its demands were legally serious and, I will say it plainly, substantially correct. The third was the fingerprint.

"Here," I said, reading it to María and Camila. "Demand three. The company must also cease all use of the phrase *el de Doña María* in commerce." I set the letter down. "Now think. The disclosure problems, any competitor's lawyer could screenshot off a phone. But that phrase. Who in the world knows the commercial value of those four words? Who tried, in a written offer, paragraph seven, to buy the names María and Doña María, forever and worldwide?"

Camila had her laptop open before I finished the question, and it took her eleven minutes and one salon owner's tagged photo to find it: a glossy sell sheet, standing in a wire rack beside a register, for a new strengthening treatment called NutriRaíz, distributed by NR Beauty Distribution LLC, and at the bottom, small, a contact line she read out loud twice. "Osvaldo Vega."

The room was quiet. On the corkboard, the warning letter and the label hung side by side, and beneath them María sat looking at nothing for a long moment, and when she finally spoke, her voice had no fear in it at all, which was new.

"Two cases a month," she said. "For five months. As if nothing happened." She smoothed the letter flat with both hands, the way she smooths final things. "He was not being kind, *Licenciado*. He was taking inventory."

"He was doing what patient men do when the front door closes," I said. "He went and built a window. And señora, before anything else, hear the part of this letter that is true, because we do not get to be wrong just because he is. The disclosures were missing. The photograph was a performance. If we ride the engagement because the engagement is good, his next letter is a lawsuit, and it names the company, and it names you, personally, because the law reaches owners who speak, and it would deserve to be taken seriously. So, the choice in front of this family is not whether he is a hypocrite. He is. It is whether we hand a hypocrite a true story to tell about us, two weeks before launch."

María looked at the sell sheet on Camila's screen, and then at her phone, face down on my table with its four hundred views inside it, and she made two decisions in one breath, and I have repeated the second one to clients ever since.

"We pull everything. Tonight. Reina, my sister, the girl in Queens, my statuses, all of it, and then you will teach every voice in this family the rules, because I will not be corrected twice." She stood and gathered her purse, and at the door she made the other decision, without raising her voice at all. "And Osvaldo's account is closed. Yes, *mija*, I know what two cases a month is worth, and I know what week it is. He is free to compete with my mother's formula. He will not do it from inside my truck."

* *

The retraining took one Sunday, one kitchen, and one laminated card, and I have since stolen the format for a dozen clients.

Camila called it *Las Reglas de la Voz*, the rules of the voice, one page, Spanish and English in two columns, in the family tradition of important paper, and every person who had ever posted, reshared, or been paid a case of product sat at María's table while she and I walked through it. Say what is true for you, always, and only what is true for you. Say what connects you, every time, in words a stranger would understand: *this is my cousin's company*, *they sent me free bottles*, *they paid me*. Never promise what the bottle may not promise, growth, cures, medicine, no matter what your own eyes saw, because your true story becomes the company's illegal claim the moment the company touches it. Never accept a script from us, because the day we write your words, your honesty stops being evidence and starts being copied. And when in doubt, before you post, one message to Camila, who answers within the hour.

Reina took it hard for exactly four minutes, until Luz, of all people, leaned over and said, "It is the baptism promise, Reina. Say it out loud where it counts," and Reina reposted her three paragraphs that night with a first line that read, *Con orgullo: la fundadora es mi prima*, with pride, the founder is my cousin, and the post performed better than the original, which taught Camila something no lawyer could have.

Doña Carmen was handled with the dignity she had earned. The video project survived, re-scoped: the company would film her story, the six years of buying, the church, the trust, her own voice in her own words, and the company's edit would carry not one syllable about growth, and nobody would hand her a script or a coaching note, and what she said to her own neighbors on her own porch was hers, free, forever, in the one voice the law does not charge for. The before-and-after photograph died without ceremony. The Queens creator reposted with the paid partnership label the platform had built for exactly this, and her comments filled with women asking where to buy, because it turns out disclosure kills nothing except the excuse.

And the numbers dipped, exactly as Camila's dashboard predicted. Reach fell by a third for eleven days, and María, to her credit, looked at the falling line every morning and did not touch her phone at two a.m., and on the twelfth day something happened that no dashboard had predicted. The owner of one of the two salons called Camila, and she was not calling about the takedowns. She was calling because in twenty years of reps and sell sheets and miracle launches, this was the first brand she had ever watched correct itself before anyone made it, and she wanted Ambarina's launch event in her salon, her chairs, her mirrors, her cost. "The other ones apologize after," she said. "Tell your mother I noticed."

"Write that down," I told Camila, and she already had, on the dashboard, in a new row she had created that day and labeled, because she is who she is, ASSETS: NON-QUANTIFIABLE (YET).

* *

My response to the downtown firm ran two pages and did three things in a fixed order, which is the whole art of answering artillery.

First, it mooted what was true: the identified posts had been removed within one business day, a written disclosure program was now in force across the company's entire speaking network, training delivered, monitoring assigned, and the file was available for inspection, which converted their best ammunition into our best exhibit. Second, it declined what was false: the phrase *el de Doña María* was a truthful, nine-year-old description of origin in the mouths of customers, the company would keep using it, and any claim to the contrary should be brought by a client willing to put its own name on the caption. And third, it opened a drawer and let them hear it open: our review of NutriRaíz's own launch materials had noted, with interest, several phrases concerning roots and follicles that we were, for the moment, merely filing. I close with the sentence that ends most of these exchanges before they become careers: *We remain available to discuss, though we suspect there is nothing to discuss.*

There was nothing to discuss. The reply, when it came, was one paragraph of lawyer for *received and noted*, and the wire racks with the sell sheets, Camila reported, quietly vanished from both salons within the month, though not, I suspected, from the wider county, and I filed that suspicion where I file things that will matter in a later chapter.

What did not vanish was the bill for being believable. This is the accounting nobody shows a family until it is theirs: substantiation is the cost of goods sold, as real as glass and caps. The claims file Camila opened that month, the structured home-use panel, thirty real customers, numbered questionnaires, signed consents, photographs under honest light, existed so that every printed word had inventory behind it, and it cost money the way inventory costs money, and it went into the spreadsheet as exactly that. Juliana, whose file-building month was running parallel to ours, sent word through the salon telegraph that she had retired the word *natural* entirely, unwinnable, and had found a laboratory to earn her the word *gentler* the expensive way, and that when it arrived it would be the only substantiated word in her whole category, which is another way of saying a moat.

On Friday evening Camila stayed late in my conference room, spreadsheet open, entering the month's new lines with her jaw set: the pulled campaign's sunk costs, the panel invoices, the two cases a month that would never be ordered again, the launch now nineteen days out.

She totaled it, looked at the number, and then scrolled left, all the way left, to a cell that had not changed since the third week of this story, the retail price, fourteen dollars, unexamined since the folding table at the church.

She created a new file and titled it EL PRECIO, and set the meeting for the following Tuesday, and in the invitation, she wrote one line to her mother and copied me, and the line said: *Profe promised us an uncomfortable afternoon. It's time.*

PART V

THE LAUNCH

CHAPTER FOURTEEN
The Real Cost of a Bottle

Alexa built the machine that ended three family arguments, and she built it, as usual, on her grandmother.

I had given her the assignment the way I gave her the interview kit months before, generic, no client, no facts. "A calculator," I said. "The true cost of one of anything. Build me a template a family business could fill in on Tuesday, and make it hunt for the costs people hide from themselves. Then test it on something with no stakes."

She tested it on flan.

"So, here's what happened," she reported Monday, dropping a printed sheet on my desk with the expression of a person who has discovered a body. "I sat with Abuela and costed one flan de coco. Eggs, condensed milk, coconut, the gas, the caramel she burns and throws away one time out of three. Total: four dollars and ten cents, and she sells them to the church bazaar people for eight, so she's rich, right? Doubling her money. Except." She tapped the sheet's center column, the one she had added at eleven at night, the one that made the template worth anything. "Four hours, Tío. Soaking, straining, the water bath, standing there watching it like it owes her money. Four hours of a human being's life, priced at zero. So, I put her time in at even a cleaning lady's wage and the eight-dollar flan costs nineteen dollars to make, and my abuela has spent thirty years paying the church bazaar eleven dollars per flan for the privilege of being praised." She sat down. "Information really is free. Flan is four hours. Every family business in Miami is running on a column nobody prints."

"Name the column," I said, "on the template, in bold, so nobody can unsee it."

She did. She named it THE HOURS NOBODY BILLS, and the template went to Camila that afternoon, blank, generic, and loaded like a mousetrap.

* *

The meeting Camila had titled EL PRECIO convened on Tuesday, and she opened it with a sentence designed to detonate on contact.

"Mamá, at fourteen dollars, once this company is honest with itself, we lose money on every bottle a salon sells. Not little money. Real money. I ran the whole thing. Do you want the funeral in pesos or dollars?"

María looked at me, and I nodded at the screen, because the arithmetic deserved to make its own argument. Camila had taken the blank template and filled it with the family's truth, line by line, and the lines told the story of everything the last thirteen chapters had built and what all of it weighed.

The bottle and cap cost sixty-two cents, and the label, Paloma's label, eighteen. Meridian's fill, for the era about to begin, ran two dollars and ninety-eight. The ingredients ran a dollar fifteen a bottle, and inside that number lived a change María had not fully absorbed yet, because for nine years the special ingredient had arrived from Medellín the way everything in that world arrives, in the suitcases of cousins, informally, lovingly, and illegally enough that nobody asked. Commercial quantities end that era, and I made the point once, plainly, so it would never need making again. A company imports the way a company does everything now, formally, with entries and a customs broker and duties paid, and the toll is priced into the bottle like glass and caps, because the alternative is building a national brand on a supply chain that cannot survive one question at an airport. Freight and boxes added thirty cents, and the safety file, the stability work, and the thirty-woman panel, amortized across the early volumes, added a quarter per bottle, substantiation as a cost of goods, exactly as promised.

And then the line that stopped the room.

"Concentrate labor," Camila read. "Fifty-five cents a bottle." She looked up at her mother. "That's you, Mamá. Your hours, in the kitchen, making the head of the recipe, priced at an honest wage. Alexa's template has a column called THE HOURS NOBODY BILLS, and when I filled it in, the biggest unpaid employee in this company's history walked out of the math, and it was you. Nine years. You never once charged the business for your own life."

"A mother does not invoice," María said, with the finality of scripture.

"Then the business eats its mother," I said, "and señora, that is not a figure of speech, it is the oldest set of books in the world. Every family company that prices the founder's hours at zero is running a hidden donation from the person who can least afford it, and the donation only becomes visible on the day she cannot work, when the company suddenly has to buy at market rate what it had been taking for free, and the price of everything turns out to have been a lie the whole time. We price your hours now, while it is cheap to be honest."

The template's verdict came next, and Camila delivered it the way surgeons deliver news, all at once. Loaded and honest, a bottle cost about six dollars and sixty-three cents to put into the world. A proper salon, and this was the second argument the spreadsheet ended, does not carry a product for two dollars of margin; the family's own salons had been doing it for years at a fraction of what the trade requires, out of love, which is why no new salon had ever said yes. Real shelves want their forty percent. Price the retail at fourteen, pay the channel honestly, and the company would collect eight dollars and forty cents a bottle against six sixty-three of cost, and then rent, insurance, marketing, and the modest salaries of its two actual employees would arrive, and the honest answer, the red number at the bottom of the column, was a loss of about one dollar and twenty-three cents on every salon bottle, forever, at any volume.

"Fourteen dollars was never a price," Camila said. "It was a feeling. It was 2016's feeling, from before Meridian, before the panel, before customs, before we paid you, from back when the whole compliance chapter of this company was a shoebox. The feeling stayed loyal to a company that doesn't exist anymore."

And the third argument ended without anyone having to win it, because the spreadsheet had one more row, and Camila had labeled it, with visible enjoyment, TÍA WAS RIGHT. "Eighteen dollars," she said.

"In New York. For nine years. We treated it like she was overcharging. She was the only person in this family pricing the product like she respected it."

* *

The number the model wanted was twenty-four dollars, and the fight that mattered was never about the number.

María heard twenty-four, and fourteen forty to the salons, and the survey data that had predicted all of it months ago, the blind guesses of eighteen and twenty-two and thirty, the niece paying thirty at the mall for something worse, and she agreed with every column, and then she took out a folded paper of her own, because she had come armed too, and hers had names on it.

"Amparo," she read. "Cleans houses in the Gables, buys two bottles a month, one for her mother in Pereira. Gloria, from the choir, fixed income. The Machado girls, three sisters, one bottle between them, they measure it." She set the list down next to the spreadsheet, paper against screen, her ledger against her daughter's. "These are not customers, *mija.* These are the women who bought from a folding table when it had no name. Now the name is beautiful, and the price says that this is no longer for you. Ten dollars more is nothing on your screen. On Amparo's Friday, it is everything. Tell me about the column for that."

The room was quiet, and I let it stay quiet, because this is the real pricing meeting, the one under the one with numbers, and every founder from a community sits in it eventually, and there is only one honest way through, which is the truth turned right side up.

"Señora, look at your list again and tell me who has been subsidizing whom. For nine years, the price stayed at fourteen for Amparo, and it also stayed at fourteen for the women in the Coral Gables chairs whose handbags cost more than your equipment, and for the customers in Queens paying your sister eighteen without blinking, and for every stranger for whom fourteen dollars reads not as kindness but as cheapness, as a question mark about what is in the bottle. The discount you meant for Amparo went mostly to people above her, and it was funded, we now know to the cent, by the one woman on the list poorer in unpaid hours than any of them. You. For nine years, señora, you have been the most generous donor to your own customer base, and the wealthiest women in it collected the most of your donation. That is what a feeling does when it tries to do a price's job. If you want to take care of Amparo, and you should, then take care of Amparo, by name, on purpose, in ways you choose, and let the price take care of the company that will still exist to serve her daughter."

María looked at her list for a long time. Then she did the thing that makes her who she is, which is to accept a hard truth and immediately improve on everyone's plan for living with it.

"Then it is twenty-four, and the price will tell the truth about why," she said. "Not a sign in the salon. A letter. From me, in Spanish and English, in the tradition of the important papers of this family, to every woman who bought from the table and the church and the kitchen. It will say what the new price pays for. The customs paid correctly. The laboratory that checks every batch. The insurance. The women in Hialeah who fill the bottles with their names on real paychecks. It will say that the price grew up because the promise grew up, and it will say thank you, and it will be true, every line. And the first hundred women, *las de la mesa*, the ones from the table, will each receive one bottle of the new one, with the new label, as a gift, from me, before launch, so that the first time they see my mother's face on it, it costs them nothing." She folded her list and put it away. "The ones who stay will stay for the truth. The ones who go were never going to like any letter."

* *

The letters went out eleven days before launch, and the ledger of what happened next is short and exact.

Of roughly one hundred seventy standing monthly buyers, fourteen did not reorder. The two salons, offered honest margin for the first time in their association with this family, both increased their commitments, and the owner who had noticed the corrections now noticed the economics, and asked, in the same call, whether Ambarina had considered other locations, because she had a cousin with two chairs in Kendall, and Camila opened a file. The sister in Queens signed the company's first formal reseller terms, prepaid, with territory and pricing written down, and her nine years of eighteen-dollar instincts converted overnight from family arbitrage into the company's first distributorship, and the paper that did it was two pages long and contained, because everything now did, a clause about payment. I made that the week's second permanent lesson: payment terms are contract terms, every one of them. The processor's fees, the chargeback rules buried in the merchant agreement, the net-thirty a retailer will someday request, all of it is somebody lending somebody money whether or not anyone used the word, and a company that does not read its payment terms is a bank that does not know it opened.

And Amparo did not come back. I record it because María records it, and because this book does not sell painless fences. Gloria stayed, with the gift bottle on her windowsill. The Machado sisters stayed and stopped measuring. But at church, in the third week, Amparo passed María at the coffee table and said, not unkindly, which made it worse, "*Ya no es para nosotras*," it is not for us anymore, and María came to the office the next morning and told me about it standing up, and did not cry, and did not take it back, and asked Camila to make sure Amparo's mother in Pereira somehow kept receiving her bottle anyway, quietly, through the cousin network, priced at nothing, filed under the only column of the spreadsheet María ever added personally, one row, in her own hand, at the bottom: LO QUE NO SE COBRA, what is not charged.

Camila let it stand, unformulated, unallocated, and when the auditors of some future chapter ask what it is, the answer in the file reads, in Camila's typing, *founder's discretion, permanent.*

* *

The last screen of the pricing model was the one that set up everything that comes next, and Camila saved it for the end of the Tuesday meeting like a good storyteller.

It was a simple chart, cash across time, and it showed a company that was, for the first time in its existence, correctly priced, honestly costed, and healthily margined, and the line still dove underwater in month three and stayed there through month five, because the second Meridian release would come due, and inventory would have to be built before wholesale checks arrived, and launches eat cash in exactly the weeks they generate applause. The trough at the bottom of the dive was circled in red, and the number inside the circle was twenty-eight thousand dollars.

"So let me make sure I understand the last nine months," María said, studying it. "We are finally profitable, and we are about to be broke."

"Welcome to growth, señora," I said. "Profit is a verdict. Cash is oxygen. They run on different clocks, and the gap between their clocks is that red circle, and next week we go shopping for oxygen, and I will warn you now, so that nothing in that chapter surprises you." I tapped the circle. "Money is never more charming than when you are twenty-eight thousand dollars short of your own success. Everyone will want to help. The bank, the family, the strangers, and somewhere out there, always, a patient man with a checkbook. The whole art is remembering what we learned at Meridian's table. The most expensive money in the world is the money you accept at the moment of maximum wanting."

Camila closed the laptop, which is how she signs things.

"Then we'd better decide our no," she said, "before we hear their yes."

CHAPTER FIFTEEN
Other People's Money

Money, it turns out, also has four doors, and I drew them on the same whiteboard where the four doors of ownership had stood eight months before, because the family had twenty-eight thousand dollars of red circle to fill and eleven days of launch runway, which is exactly the combination that makes people stop reading what they sign.

"Door one, family and friends. The warmest money and the most flammable, because it is never only money. Door two, debt. A bank, a rate, a schedule, and, for companies this size, a signature that follows you home. Door three, equity. A stranger buys a piece of the company itself, forever, and the price is never only the percentage. And door four, the one everyone forgets because it does not look like financing at all. Customers. Money paid in advance for products not yet delivered is the cheapest capital on earth. It carries no interest, surrenders no ownership, and costs only a promise, which is the one currency this family has never devalued." I capped the marker. "We are going to knock on all four this week, and before we do, hear the house rule. Every dollar has a price, and the price is never printed on the dollar. It is printed in the interest, the equity, the control, and the relationships, and our job is to read all four prices before the wanting starts. Because you are about to learn what twenty-eight thousand short of your own success feels like, and I promise you, señora, you have never been more attractive in your life."

The first door knocked on us before we could knock on it.

His name was Chucho, a cousin on the Restrepo side, a man who had built a towing company from one truck to nine and wore the story on a gold chain, and he came to Sunday dinner with an envelope and love in his eyes and offered thirty thousand dollars across the *sancocho.* No papers, he said. Family does not sign with family. Just remember me when it is big.

María told me about it Monday, and then she told me what she had answered, and I wrote it down while she spoke because some clients eventually begin practicing law back at you.

"I said, Chucho, I love you, and I have already paid forty thousand dollars on Sundays to learn what those words cost. If your money comes, it comes on paper, with a number, a date, and what happens if we fail, written down, so that in five years we are still eating at the same table no matter what happens to the company. And he laughed and patted my hand and said, María, you have been spending too much time with lawyers." She folded her hands. "So, there is no cousin money, *Licenciado.* He was not offering an investment. He was offering a debt with no terms, which you taught me is the same as a debt with every term, decided later, by the angrier person."

"There is one more reason it goes on paper, señora, and I want it in the family's permanent memory. When a company takes money from anyone, even a cousin, even at dinner, the law calls the thing being sold a security, and there is no family exemption from the securities laws. There are lawful lanes for small private raises, and every one of those lanes still forbids the thing families do most naturally, which is to promise. The moment anyone says, you will double it, you cannot lose, this thing is guaranteed, the speaker has left the world of dinner and entered the world of fraud, with cousins as witnesses. Papered, disclosed, honest, or not at all."

* *

The bank was door two, and the bank said yes so pleasantly that Camila almost missed what the yes was holding.

The offer was a thirty-thousand-dollar line at a rate that made her wince but not bleed and attached to it were two documents that I made the family read at my conference table at the speed of the old country. The first was the security agreement, and its collateral clause was the sentence banks have been quietly perfecting for a century: a lien on all assets of the company, inventory, receivables, equipment, and general intangibles, now owned or hereafter acquired.

"General intangibles," Camila read. "That's IP. Profe, that's the trademark. That's the patent application." She looked up. "If we default, the bank takes Abuela?"

"Read the architecture before you panic, and then never forget why the architecture exists. What does the company own?" I waited, because she had earned the arriving of it. "The company owns bottles, a bank account, some receivables, two molds in a fortress in Doral, and a license. The formula is not in the building. It never was. It sits with your mother, personally, exactly where we put it the week this company was born, on the day I told you the crown jewels do not live in the room where the fighting happens. The bank's lien reaches everything the company owns and nothing the company borrows, and the most valuable thing in this enterprise is, by design, borrowed from María. This is the day the boring paragraph from Chapter One of this company pays for itself. We will still negotiate the lien down to inventory and receivables, because banks price fear they do not need, but even at its widest, the fence held before the wolf arrived."

The second document was one page, and it was the one I slowed the room down for, because it was the one with María's name on it alone. The personal guarantee.

"This paper is different from every paper you have signed in this story, señora, and I will not let it be signed the way papers get signed. Everything else bound the company. This binds you. If the company cannot pay, the bank may come past the wall we built, to your accounts, your savings, the things with your name on them, and no clever structure changes that, because that is the entire purpose of the page, and the bank will not lend without it, and they are not villains for asking. Small companies borrow on their founders' backs. That is the market. So, the only question is whether the founder walks in with her eyes open." I slid it across. "Read it to me. Out loud. All of it. And where the English resists you, I will translate, and we do not sign today. We sign Thursday, after you have slept on it twice."

She read it aloud, all of it, stopping four times for translation, and when she finished, she looked at the page for a moment and then at me.

"You do this with everyone? The reading out loud?"

"With everyone, señora, since long before you. Years ago, I signed papers I should have read first, and I have stood on both sides of tables like this one, and that is all that story needs to be for now. The ceremony is not for the bank. It is for the Thursday version of you, so that whatever happens in the next five years, there will never be a morning when you can say to yourself, I did not know what that page was."

On Thursday she signed it, a line sized down to fifteen thousand, the lien negotiated to inventory and receivables, and she asked for a copy for her purse, and I understood by then that María's purse was where this family kept its treaties.

* *

The angel came through the third door wearing the nicest suit in this book, and he came for Camila.

His name was Marcos Ferrer, he invested in what he called overlooked founders and authentic brands, and he had watched the corrected campaign, the disclosed reposts, the letter that told customers the truth about a price, and he used the word *integrity* the way other men use cologne. He took the family to lunch. He took Camila, separately, to coffee, and spoke of CFO tracks and his network and rooms she deserved to be in, and I want to record plainly that nothing he said was false, which is what made him dangerous, and that two days later Camila walked into my office with a term sheet and a memo she had written at two in the morning arguing that we should take it.

Sixty thousand dollars for thirty percent, the memo said, solves the trough four times over, funds Kendall, funds the metered bottle's second release, and buys a mentor with a Rolodex. She had modeled it. The model glowed.

"Then let us read the term sheet the way I read depositions," I said, "which is not for what it says. For what it is preparing to say later. Page one, the board. Three seats, one of them his, with a schedule of decisions requiring his consent. New products, budgets over ten thousand, hiring, and, item six, any transaction with a related party. Camila, name this company's largest related-party transaction."

She saw it before she finished the question forming. "The license. Mamá's license. The formula."

"Item six makes your grandmother's formula a conflict of interest requiring Marcos Ferrer's annual approval. Now page three, the diligence conditions, and here is the sentence the whole document was built to deliver. 'Prior to closing, the company shall acquire full ownership of all intellectual property currently licensed from founders.' He is not asking to invest beside the fence, *mija*. He is asking, as a condition of his money, that the fence be dismantled and the crown jewels moved into the one building he will hold a veto over. And page four. The redemption right. Read it as an accountant, not an admirer."

She read it twice, and I watched the two-in-the-morning memo die behind her eyes. "After year three, he can force the company to buy back his shares at one and a half times what he paid." She did the arithmetic she was born doing. "That's not equity. Equity means he wins if we win and loses if we lose. This wins either way. If we succeed, he owns thirty percent of a success. If we stall, he pulls a ripcord and we owe him ninety thousand dollars we would not have, which means the company gets sold or gutted to pay him." She set the pages down. "It's a loan wearing equity's clothes, at fifty percent interest, with a board seat and a key to the vault."

María, who had listened to the entire autopsy without a word, asked the only two questions she ever needs.

"What does he get if we fail?"

"Paid," Camila said. "From the furniture."

"And what must we give up on the first day, before any of the winning or failing?"

"The formula," I said. "Into the reachable building."

She nodded slowly, the way she nods when a shape she has seen before comes around again. "Osvaldo offered forty thousand for everything and called it a purchase. This one offers sixty for everything and calls it a partnership." She gathered her purse. "He is Osvaldo who went to college. Tell him no with beautiful manners, *Licenciado*. And *mija*." She stopped at the door, and what she said next she said gently, because she had stood in that exact wind herself, at a different table, with a pen already in her hand. "He did not lie to you. The rooms are real and you do deserve them. But you wrote that memo at two in the morning, and nothing signed at two in the morning has ever made this family richer. We decided on a Tuesday, remember. In the calm."

I told Marcos no with beautiful manners. He took it like a professional, wished us well like a professional, and at the very end, standing, permitted himself one sentence off the professional script. "Everyone takes the money eventually, counselor. Call me at the trough." Which told me he had read the same chart we had and had been pricing the red circle all along.

* *

So, the family filled the circle through the fourth door, the one that does not look like financing, and it took nine days and no strangers.

Camila built the pre-order, and she built it the way this family now built everything, with the promises priced before the posts went up. Four hundred and ten women paid twenty-four dollars in advance for a bottle of Ambarina to be delivered at launch, under terms that said plainly, in both languages, what was bought, when it would arrive, and how a change of mind would be refunded, because customer money is borrowed money and the loan documents are your own checkout page. The Queens distributorship prepaid its opening order, which its new two-page contract had priced in from the beginning. Ingrid, asked whether the second Meridian release could breathe two months later, moved it with one email and one sentence, *we make room for clients who walked out of here once*, which I have added to my private file of reasons the fortress was worth it. And the fifteen-thousand-dollar line sat behind all of it, mostly undrawn, the way oxygen is supposed to sit behind a dive.

Camila ran the new chart at the end of the week. The red circle had become a shallow dip that never touched the waterline, and underneath it she had typed the epitaph of the sixty thousand dollars: *needed 28, offered 60, took 0 from strangers.* The cost of the smaller way was real and she printed that too. Launch inventory thinner by a third, Kendall delayed a quarter, one founder's signature promising the bank her own kitchen table. Nobody called it free. Everybody signed it anyway, in the calm, on a Tuesday.

Eleven days remained. The salon was booked, the mirrors were promised, four hundred and ten bottles were spoken for by name, and across town, according to my niece, a young man had rented a rooftop and a fog machine for what he was calling the MAX Experience, scheduled, with the algorithm's sense of humor, for the very same Saturday a woman from Medellín was going to stand in a salon in her mother's neighborhood and sell the first bottle that had ever carried the family's real name.

Two launches would share one Saturday. One of them had a fog machine. The other one had four hundred and ten receipts.

CHAPTER SIXTEEN
Launch Day

The week before launch, my niece read the agreements nobody on earth reads and came out of them like a diver coming up with wreckage.

I had assigned it the usual way, generic, no client, no facts: take the standard click-through agreements of the commerce world, the website builders, the payment processors, the marketplaces, and give me a plain-language map of what a founder actually signs when she checks the little box. Alexa spent two nights inside the fine print and arrived Monday with a memo she had titled, with her gift for titles, WHAT THE BOX SAYS.

"Section nine, Tío. There's always a section nine. The free website builder takes a license to upload everything you upload, your photos, your logo, your grandmother's face, worldwide, royalty-free, for operating and promoting the service. You still own it, fine, but you've licensed it to a landlord you've never met, and nobody knows, because nobody reads. The payment processor is better. The payment processor can hold your money. If refunds spike, if chargebacks cross a threshold, if their risk software has a bad dream about you, they can freeze the account, keep a reserve for ninety days, and the agreement you clicked says you agreed. Your revenue, their custody, their timeline." She dropped the memo on my desk. "You told me in week one that I felt hired when you made me sign something. Update: I've now read what the whole internet makes everybody sign, and I finally understand this office. The costume was never on the paperwork. The costume is on the checkbox."

The memo became a checklist, and the checklist crossed the wall the lawful way, as counsel to the client, and Camila spent the week building the checkout the way this family now built everything. Terms of sale in both languages said what a customer bought, when it would ship, and how a change of mind came back, because the pre-order chapter had already taught them that the checkout page is a loan document. A privacy notice told the truth in one page: we collect your name, your address, your number if you give it, we use them to deliver bottles and send news you asked for, we sell them to no one, ever, and here is how you make us forget you. And the WhatsApp chains, the beating heart of the whole distribution, came inside the fence: news sent only to women who had said yes, with a way out printed at the bottom of every message, because a community built on trust does not get to market like a spammer just because the messages are in Spanish and the sender is somebody's *comadre*.

"One more thing," Alexa said, at the door, off the record, which is where she keeps her real questions now. "The processor freeze clause. That's not theoretical, right? That happens to real people."

"It happens," I said, "almost always to people who find out what they signed on the worst possible night to find out."

She wrote something down, and I did not know yet that the week was going to grade her memo in public.

* *

The crisis came Friday night, as crises contractually must, and I received it Saturday morning as an artifact: Camila's phone, handed across the salon's front counter, open to a text thread stamped between 1:12 and 1:56 a.m.

The thread began with an inventory of everything that was not perfect. The Spanish half of the website had four pages still in English. The founder video was uncolored. Sixty of Romero's two thousand labels had gone on by hand at a two-degree tilt that nobody on the planet would notice except the person who had commissioned the artwork. The metered bottle, the crown, was months away, so the launch would be the classic only, which at 1:30 in the morning had begun to feel to Camila like opening a museum with one wing. The thread proposed, at 1:41, in the reasonable voice exhaustion always borrows, pushing the launch one week, just one, to get it right.

María's reply arrived at 1:56 a.m., and it was complete at sixteen words, and Camila had screenshotted it, which is how her generation frames things.

Mija. My mother launched this in 1962 with a pot and no lid. Push the button.

The button got pushed at 1:58. The site went live with four pages in the wrong language and sixty crooked labels, and I recorded the imperfections deliberately, in the permanent file, because of what they turned out to weigh, which was nothing. No customer ever found the four pages. The crooked labels sold in the first two hours, and one of them, I am told, was requested specifically, by a woman who heard about the tilt on WhatsApp and wanted a bottle that proved human hands.

"Perfect is a place you polish toward after you exist," I told Camila when I handed the phone back. "It has never once been an address you launch from."

* *

The salon opened at ten, and by five minutes before the hour the sidewalk outside held more women than the fire code technically contemplated, and María could not walk out of the back room.

I found her there because I had gone looking, past the mirrors and the borrowed chairs, and she was standing with her back to the shelf of amber bottles, in her best dress, holding one bottle in both hands the way she had held the first one on my desk a year and a lifetime ago, and her breathing was doing what breathing does before public courage.

"Nine years I sold this," she said, not really to me. "From the kitchen, from the table, from the trunk of the car. Never once was I afraid. And now there is a sign with my mother's face on it, and a line on the sidewalk, and my legs have decided to be seventy years old." She looked at me. "What is different, *Licenciado*? Tell me legally what is different."

"Legally, señora, nothing. The same product, the same law, the same you. What is different is that today it carries your family's real name, in public, where failing would also have a name. That fear is not a malfunction. That fear is the entry fee of standing behind something out loud, and every founder who ever mattered paid it at a door like this one, and not one of them will tell you it stopped. They will only tell you what Camila's grandmother would tell you." I nodded at the door, where the noise of the sidewalk was coming through like weather. "The pot never had a lid, señora. Out you go."

She went out, and the room did what rooms do for a woman like that, and I stepped back against the wall where lawyers belong at parties and watched a launch happen in concentric circles, exactly as drawn on a whiteboard months before, except alive. The innermost ring, *las de la mesa*, the women of the folding table, arrived holding their gift bottles like passports, and Gloria from the choir had brought hers back photographed on her windowsill, printed, in a frame, as a present for María, which is a sentence I am not able to improve. Doña Carmen held a corner of the salon all afternoon, unfilmed, unscripted, uncoached, telling her story to one circle of strangers after another in the one voice the law never charges for, and I watched women listen to her and then walk to the register, and I thought about the meeting where a furious, honest girl told me the mealy words were beneath the truth, and how the truth had found its lawful mouth after all. Reina worked the room with her phone out and her disclosure in her bio like a medal. Luz ran the stockroom like a customs checkpoint. The salon owner, the one who noticed, stood behind her own register ringing up another woman's brand at cost, shaking her head happily at the arithmetic of trust.

At the church, four blocks away, where a second table handled the overflow of the neighborhood, Camila went at noon to restock and came back quiet, and pulled her mother behind the mirrors, and showed her a photograph on her phone. It was the folding table, the original, nine years old, the one from the sales history, with the cracked leg that had been failing since spring. Somebody had come in the early morning, before the church opened, and repaired it, with new wood on the broken leg, sanded, stained close to the old color, the work of a man who owned his own tools and did not need to be asked twice or thanked once. There was no note. Nobody had seen anyone.

María looked at the photograph for a long time. She touched the screen once, where the new wood met the old, and she did not say the name, and neither did Camila, and neither will I. Some signatures are not for the file.

A stranger at the register asked her, late in the afternoon, the question the whole apparatus had been trained for. "Be honest with me. Does it really make your hair grow?" And María, radiant, dangerous, nine years of testimony sitting in her mouth like a loaded choir, smiled and delivered the sentence exactly as designed. "Señora, I am the seller, so I will only tell you what I may. It made seventy years of customers come back. For the rest, ask them." She gestured at Carmen's corner, and the stranger went, listened, and bought three.

* *

Across town, the MAX Experience had a rooftop, a fog machine, a countdown clock, and, as of 8:40 that evening, a problem that arrived exactly the way problems arrive in section nine.

Alexa fed me the updates in the manner of a courtroom sketch artist, from the front desk of her phone, public feeds only. The event itself was enormous. Two thousand people attended, with a drone, influencers in matching orange, and Victor descending a staircase to his own theme music with the confidence of a man whose comment section he had stopped reading. The livestream peaked at forty thousand watching. And then, at 8:40, with the fog machine at full commitment, the checkout died. Card after card declined on camera, the pinned link spun, and within minutes the chat solved the mystery faster than the host could, because somebody in it had received the same email other merchants receive on the worst possible night: payments paused pending review, funds reserved, reference your merchant agreement.

"Chargebacks," Alexa said quietly, watching. "Day thirty came for five thousand customers, the refunds spiked, the risk software had its bad dream, and the clause did what the clause says. His revenue, their custody, their timeline. He's finding out what he signed live, in fog, in front of forty thousand people." She looked up at me. "And that's not even the part I'd be scared of, if I were him. Scroll his tags."

I scrolled his tags. The top post of the evening was not about the checkout. It was a photograph, taken that afternoon in a beauty-supply store in Hialeah by someone with an ordinary phone and an excellent eye: two serum bottles side by side on a shelf, same bottle, same cap, same fill line, one wearing flames and one wearing a volcano, with a caption that asked, in two languages, the question a showroom had asked us months ago in glass and silence. *¿El mismo producto?* The same product? It had eleven thousand shares and was reproducing.

The first crack never looks like the collapse. It looks like a payment error and a photograph, on the biggest night, in the smallest font.

* *

The family counted the day at María's kitchen table at eleven that night, all of them, Luz with her shoes off, Reina asleep sitting up, the radio low.

Six hundred and eighty bottles had left the building between the salon, the church, and the website, against a launch inventory deliberately thinned by the price of keeping the company, and Camila read the numbers out loud like psalms, the sell-through rates, the Kendall salon owner's cousin who had come in person and left a card, the four hundred and ten pre-orders now boxed for Monday's mail. María listened to all of it with her hands around a coffee she was drinking, and the vertigo of the morning was gone, replaced by the specific exhausted stillness of a person who jumped and was caught.

It was 11:52 when Camila's phone chimed, and she glanced at it out of habit, and then she did not put it down.

"Mamá," she said. "*Ven.*"

She set the phone in the middle of the table, among the cups, and turned the screen so everyone could see it, and nobody said anything, because there was nothing to add and everything to understand. Four hundred and ten orders had come from women whose mothers they knew, whose churches they knew, whose sisters carried bottles in suitcases. This was the next number, and it belonged to no circle they had ever drawn.

NEW ORDER #411 CONFIRMED
Ambarina Strengthening Formula, 1 × $24.00
K. Whitfield, Tulsa, Oklahoma

PART VI

THE GROWTH

CHAPTER SEVENTEEN
The Wholesale Question

The chain found them twenty-two days after Tulsa, which is about how long it takes a category manager to notice a line at a salon and a photograph reproducing on the internet.

Costa Beauty Supply ran twenty-three stores from Homestead to Vero, and its buyer, a brisk and genuinely friendly woman named Yvette, did the seduction the way the good ones do it, with a picture instead of a promise. She met María and Camila at the flagship store and walked them to the hair-care aisle, and there, printed full size and taped over the existing shelf, was a planogram mockup her team had prepared: Ambarina, amber and gold, Marta's face at eye level, four facings wide, in twenty-three windows across the bottom half of Florida.

María stood in front of it for a long moment, and she told me about that moment afterward with the honesty I have come to bank on. "My mother sold from a table, *Licenciado*. And there was her face, at the height of my eyes, in a store with automatic doors. I felt it in my chest like a hand. I would have signed the shelf itself if she had handed me a pen in that aisle." She said it without shame, which is the only way that sentence is ever useful. "That is why we have the rule about the calm. Because the aisle is not the calm."

The terms arrived by email that evening, nine pages wearing a friendly cover note, and Camila printed them, and we performed the autopsy at my conference table the next morning under the corkboard, the way this family now met all beautiful strangers.

"Start with the price, because everything else is decoration on the price. They pay ten dollars and eighty cents a bottle." Camila had the model open before I finished the sentence. "Our loaded cost is six twenty-five. So, four fifty-five gross, before what comes next, and what comes next is the whole nine pages. A slotting fee, eight thousand five hundred dollars, for the privilege of the shelf, payable at signing. A five percent advertising co-op deducted off every invoice for flyers we will never see. A two percent damage allowance, deducted whether anything is damaged or not. Payment at ninety days, which means we finance their inventory for a fiscal quarter with a bank line Mamá guaranteed with her kitchen table. And this one." She flattened the page. "Guaranteed sale. Anything that does not sell, they return, whenever, for full credit, freight ours. Profe, that's not a purchase order. We hold the inventory risk, they hold the shelf, and if the product sits, the whole donation comes home in a truck we pay for."

"Now the trap door," I said, because every form has one, and this form's trap door was on page seven. "Termination for convenience, thirty days, any reason or none. Read it next to the requirement two pages earlier that the supplier maintains dedicated inventory for all twenty-three stores at all times. So, the family builds and warehouses a chain-sized stockpile as a contractual duty, and the chain may walk away from the arrangement in thirty days on a Tuesday, whereupon the stockpile becomes a monument. And then the sentence that decides everything, page eight. Exclusivity, retail, state of Florida." I let them read it themselves, because some clauses should arrive in the reader's own voice. "Signing this closes the salons. The owner who gave you her mirrors at cost. The Kendall cousin. The stockist agreements we have been drafting. The whole trust network that built this company would be contractually converted into a violation of it."

The room was quiet, and I gave them the frame that the nine pages had been designed to prevent anyone from reaching.

"Here is what I want this family to understand before any counteroffer, because it is the actual lesson and the clause-by-clause is only evidence. Wholesale to a chain is not your business grown larger. It is a different business wearing your product. Until now you have sold bottles to women. This contract proposes that you finance a retailer's inventory, insure its markdowns, rent its eye-level real estate, and staff a receivables department, all denominated in bottles. Some companies should do exactly that, at the right terms, at the right size, on purpose. What no company should ever do is wander into that business by accident because a buyer taped a beautiful picture over a shelf. So, we will answer the way we answer, and we will find out which conversation this really is."

The counter went out under my signature and it was short: real margin at fourteen forty; no exclusivity in any geography; net thirty; no guaranteed sale, replaced with a first-order markdown contribution, capped, because we do not pretend retail carries no risk, we merely decline to carry all of it; slotting credited back against the first year's orders, so that the shelf is an advance and not a toll; and reciprocal termination at sixty days with a sell-off period.

Yvette called me herself, which I respected, and passed, which I had expected, and on her way off the phone she left the sentence that told me the rest of the season's story in advance. "No hard feelings, counselor, it's a good little brand. We have a comparable line already at our economics, so the set's covered either way. *Nutri* something." She said it the way buyers say things, already three calls ahead, and I wrote the word down and drew a box around it and sat for a moment with the shape of what had just happened.

* *

I told María at the Thursday meeting, plainly, because she had earned plain. The twenty-three windows would be filled, four facings wide, by NutriRaíz, at ten eighty a bottle, with the slotting fee, the co-op, the ninety days, the guaranteed sale, and the trapdoor, all of it, signed by a man with a checkbook and a patience I no longer underestimated.

She absorbed it the way she absorbs things now, and I watched the ego take its hit honestly, without pretending it was not an ego. "So, Osvaldo gets the windows," she said. "And the automatic doors. And my mother stays on the folding table." She smoothed the printout of the planogram, which she had kept, because of course she had kept it. "Tell me why I should not feel like we lost, *Licenciado*, and do not be gentle."

"Then here is ungentle. Run his deal through your daughter's spreadsheet. At their economics, every bottle he ships to those shelves loses money before it sells and loses more if it does not, and he has agreed to warehouse for twenty-three stores against a thirty-day trapdoor, financed at ninety days, in a category where his product has no choir. No church, no Carmen, no *comadres*, no seventeen women who cried in folding chairs. A shelf does not tell stories, señora. It just charges rent. What Osvaldo purchased last week, with real money, is the privilege of learning in public what you learned in this office for free: that visibility is a cost center until trust makes it an asset. Sometimes the finest move available in a market is to let your rival win the hill that drains him. We did not lose the windows. We declined to donate through them, and the donation found another donor."

María looked at the planogram one more time. Then she folded it in half and then in half again, the way she folds final things, and put it in her purse, and I understood that it was going wherever the guaranteed copy lived, in the archive of prices considered and not paid.

"The table, then," she said. "But bigger, and on paper. Show me the machine."

* *

The machine was the company's own stockist agreement, four pages, bilingual, and building it was the week's real work, because the independents were already calling and the family was done improvising channels.

Camila and I drafted it as a kit of promises running in both directions, and I will record its load-bearing walls, because they are the walls of every brand that intends to still own itself in twenty years. Territory came named and non-exclusive, so that no handshake ever again implied a kingdom. Pricing carried discipline: the suggested retail printed, and a floor policy beneath it, announced by the company and enforced by the company, because a stockist who buys customers by burning our margin is renting our brand to destroy it, and the price integrity that lets the salons live is itself an asset with a fence. Brand standards came next, and this was the clause I made María read twice, because it is the one that protects the name at the trademark office and not just the shelf: how the product may be displayed; that it may never be repackaged, rebottled, or relabeled; rotation by lot; storage out of the sun; and the company's right to walk in, look, and, if the standards fail, leave with its brand, because a name whose owner does not police how it appears eventually belongs to how it appears. Payment terms were earned, not granted, prepaid for the courtship and net fifteen after three clean orders, because trust in this family is compounded, never assumed. Termination ran reciprocal thirty days with an orderly sell-off, so that goodbyes have furniture. And one clause covered a problem that had not happened yet, planted the way fences get planted, before the animal exists: no resale on third-party marketplaces, and no shipments outside the territory, because the day was coming, I told them, when bottles would start walking to places nobody sent them, and we would be very glad the paper already had an opinion.

Three independents signed it in eleven days. The Kendall cousin, who negotiated exactly one term, her delivery window, and paid the prepay by check before the ink settled. A shop in Hialeah four blocks from Romero's, whose owner had watched the crooked-label story travel through the neighborhood and concluded, correctly, that a brand whose customers request the imperfect bottles is a brand with a choir. And a salon in Westchester that came, unprompted, on the recommendation of a woman with an anti-gray rinse and thirty-four years of marriage, because my clients had gone on finding each other in the wild, and had begun, without any instruction from me, to behave like an economy.

All three paid on time. I note it here the way Camila noted it in the dashboard, in its own row, because after nine pages of co-ops and trap doors, *paid on time* had revealed itself to be what it always was, the most beautiful term in commercial law.

* *

Doña Rosa came back on a Friday, and she did not come back as a mirror. She came back as a machine.

She had done the four pages. She had done considerably more than the four pages. In the months since a label had kept her up at night, the salon had become a company with articles and an operating agreement, the nephew who painted the sign in 2009 had signed, over an excellent lunch she described in detail, the assignment nobody had thought to ask him for in fifteen years, and her salon's name now sat in the national queue as an application, filed, dated, hers. She laid the filing receipt on my desk beside her signed stockist agreement, because that was the other reason she had come: the Coral Gables chairs wanted Ambarina, at full wholesale, prepaid, as the brand's first door into the zip codes where handbags outprice equipment.

She read the stockist agreement completely, at my table, unhurried, moving her finger under the lines the way careful readers do, and she negotiated exactly one term. Deliveries on Tuesdays, never Mondays, because Mondays were blowouts and a delivery during blowouts was an insult to both. I redlined it while she watched, and she watched the redline the way other people watch surgery, and when she signed, she sat back and looked at her own signature with a small, private astonishment.

"Twenty-two years I said my brand was my hands," she said. "You cannot register hands. *Bueno.*" She tapped the little pile, the receipt, the agreement, the assignment. "Now the hands have a filing cabinet."

The door her chairs opened did not take a week to matter. That Sunday, one of her clients, a woman I will not name because this book does not name them, posted a photograph from her own bathroom, marble and morning light, the amber bottle standing among things that cost more than the amber bottle, with a one-word caption in the universal language of that world: *obsessed.* No payment, no gift, no connection, a customer who had bought a bottle at Rosa's because she liked it, which is the one kind of endorsement no rule on earth restricts, because it is simply a person telling the truth in public.

Camila found it within the hour, of course, and what she did next is why I am recording the incident at all. She did not repost it. She screenshotted it, sent it to me with the message *material connection: none that*

I can find. Post claims: aesthetic only, no efficacy. Request: repost with credit?, and waited for the answer before touching anything, and the answer was yes, and the repost said, with permission and with credit, exactly what the original said, which was nothing except *obsessed*, which is everything. The system I wrote in the file is no longer something I run. It is something they run past me, which is the only version of a compliance program that survives its lawyer.

* *

The week closed with an inventory count at the apartment, because three stockists and a Coral Gables door meant the Romero reorder had landed, two thousand more classic bottles, cases stacked four high by the balcony, and the family counted them into the log the way the fence required, lot numbers, quantities, dates.

It was Luz who stopped, somewhere in the third stack. She had opened a case to spot-check, lifted a bottle, uncapped it the way she had uncapped ten thousand, and held it under her nose a half second longer than the motion needed.

"María," she said. "*Ven un momento.*" Come a moment.

María came, and smelled, and frowned the smallest available frown, and smelled again. "It is fine," she said slowly. "It is almost completely fine." She capped it, held the bottle up to the balcony light, tilted it, watched the way it moved. "Half a note low. The green is half a note low, and it walks down the glass a little slow." She looked at Luz, and the two women had one of their conversations without words, and then she did what the machine now existed for. She set the bottle aside on the counter, alone, and said, "Camila. Write down the lot number. Probably it is nothing."

Camila wrote down the lot number.

It was not nothing.

CHAPTER EIGHTEEN
The Batch

The golden sample was unsealed on a Tuesday morning, with witnesses, on camera, exactly as the paper had always intended, and I want to record that nobody in the room treated it lightly, because everyone in the room understood what the breaking of that seal meant. It meant the future argument had arrived.

The bottle stood on María's kitchen counter next to its suspect, the flagged bottle from lot R-242, and Neto Romero attended by video from Hialeah with his father behind his shoulder like a portrait of the previous century. Camila read the protocol aloud from the agreement, because the agreement had one, written months ago at a conference table for a day everyone had hoped would stay theoretical. María broke the seal her own signature crossed, poured the reference and the suspect side by side into glass, and did what three generations of noses had been trained to do, and then Luz did it after her, independently, in silence.

"The reference is my mother," María said at last, formally, for the camera and the record. "The other one is a stranger doing her voice." She tilted the two glasses against the light. "And it walks slowly. Half a note low, a half step slow. Neto, with respect. Something in the body of this lot is not what we approved of."

Neto's instruments, he said carefully, had read the lot at the edge of tolerance but inside it, and he said it the way an honest man reports a fact he no longer trusts, and this is the exact collision the machine had been built for, the day the numbers pass and the nose objects. So, the machine answered it. Sealed aliquots of the reference and the suspect went to the named laboratory that same afternoon, under the tiebreaker clause, loser pays the testing, and while the science traveled, the family confronted the part of the morning that could not wait for science.

Some of the lot had already shipped.

Camila had the answer in forty minutes, because the answer had been designed into everything, the lot numbers on every label, the rotation clause in every stockist agreement, the order records behind every checkout. Lot R-242 had run a thousand bottles. Five hundred twenty sat quarantined by the balcony. Four hundred eighty were in the world, and she could name where every one of them had gone: two hundred sixty across the four stockists, a hundred forty-eight through the website, seventy-two through the church and salon tables, each with a name, an address, or a shelf attached. The stranger in Tulsa, she confirmed before anyone asked, had shipped from the launch run, weeks earlier, a different lot entirely. "Traceability isn't paperwork," she said, staring at her own report with something like awe. "It's a map of exactly how sorry you're going to have to be."

* *

The argument happened that afternoon, and I am going to record it fairly, because the losing side of it was not stupid, and the instinct it argued from lives in every executive who has ever watched a good month wobble.

"Play devil's advocate with me," Camila said, pacing my conference room. "The lot is at the edge of spec but inside it, per the only instruments that have measured it so far. The difference is a half note of scent and a viscosity drift that literally two people on earth can detect, and both are related to the reference. Nobody has complained. If we pull four hundred eighty bottles out of the market six weeks after launch, we torch the momentum, we spook four stockists we just signed, we eat nine thousand dollars we budgeted for growth, and we do it all on the strength of a nose. A sacred nose. But a nose." She stopped pacing. "Explain to me why we would not wait for the lab, quietly, and decide with data."

"Because containment and explanation run on different clocks," I said, "and you have the order backward. Explanation is a luxury that contains problems can afford. An uncontained problem does not wait politely while you research it. Every day those bottles sit on shelves, the question changes from what is wrong with the batch to what did the company know and when did it stop shipping, and I have sat in the rooms where that second question gets asked, under oath, with the shipping records on the screen, and I promise you the words *we were waiting for the lab* have never once made that room go better. In this arena, Camila, the law does not grade intentions. A product either was defective and reached someone or it was not, and the only thing a company fully controls is how fast it stopped."

"One data point," Camila said. "That's my whole argument. We have zero customer complaints and one nose."

The mailbox answered her.

It arrived while she was mid-sentence, with the algorithmic timing this family's story specializes in, an email to the address printed on every label because a law had required it and María had wanted it anyway. A customer in Kendall, polite, apologetic, sorry to bother anyone. She had used the new bottle Thursday, and her scalp had itched and gone red for two days; it was better now with a cream from the pharmacy; probably it was nothing, probably it was her; but the label said to write, so she was writing. Camila read it out loud, and the room got very quiet, and Camila cross-checked the order number against her own map, already knowing.

"Lot R-242," she said.

María stood up. She was not dramatic about it. She gathered her purse the way she does when a meeting is over whether anyone else knows it yet.

"We are done discussing," she said. "One woman wrote to my mother's label to apologize for her own scalp. There is no spreadsheet under that, *mija*, and there is no lab result that makes it smaller. The bottles come home today. All of them. And nobody who bought one hears it from a letter." She looked at her daughter, and she said the thing gently, because she had stood in Camila's exact wind before, holding a pen at a fortress table. "You were not wrong about the data. You were wrong about the clock. Now get me the list, because we are going to call four hundred eighty people, and I am calling Kendall first."

* *

I will summarize the law of that week the way I summarized it for them, plainly, because the family executed all of it and deserved to know the names of what they were doing.

What they conducted was a voluntary market withdrawal, the quiet, honorable cousin of a recall, undertaken on the company's own initiative for a quality deviation before anyone required it. The customer's email was logged the day it arrived, in the record the law requires the company to keep, and it was assessed against the definitions the law cares about, and a two-day irritation resolved with a pharmacy cream did not meet the threshold that triggers a mandatory report to the government, and the file says so, with the analysis attached, because the day anyone ever asks, the answer will be a page and not a shrug. The duty that did apply was older and simpler than any statute, the duty not to keep shipping what you have reason to distrust, and the withdrawal discharged it by sundown Wednesday. And I did one more thing that week that nobody asked for, and no customer will ever see, which is that I sent notice to the company's insurer, describing the lot, the withdrawal, and the single reported reaction, resolved. Camila asked why we would wave a flag at our own insurance company over a closed complaint, and the answer is a clause and a graveyard. Every policy contains a notice provision, and late notice is how optimists lose coverage they paid for. You report the smoke, always, precisely so that the one time it turns out to be a fire, no adjuster on earth can say you hid it. Insurance is not a product you buy. It is a relationship you maintain, and the premium is candor.

The calls took three days, divided among María, Camila, and Luz, in two languages, from the kitchen table, working down Camila's map. The script was one index card long and it was mostly forbidden from being a script: say what happened, in plain words, before they ask; the batch is not what the family approved; nothing dangerous has been established and one mild reaction has been reported and resolved; bring or send the bottle back, replacement or refund, their choice, freight ours; and thank you. María took Kendall first, as promised, and stayed on the phone with the woman who had apologized for her own scalp for forty minutes, most of it, per Luz's eavesdropping, about the woman's daughters, and by the end the woman had refused the refund, accepted the replacement, and been reimbursed for the pharmacy cream, fourteen dollars, receipt photographed for the file, offered before she could think to ask.

Rosa, informed on a Tuesday because contracts are contracts, was silent on the phone for a moment and then said, "Twenty-two years in that chair, *Licenciado*, and no brand ever called me before I noticed. They call after. They call when it is on the news. Tell María her forty bottles are already in the back room, and my Tuesday delivery can bring the good ones." The Hialeah shop reordered on the same call as its return. Kendall's owner asked, carefully, whether she could tell customers why the shelf had a gap, and was told yes, tell them exactly the truth, and reported back that the truth had sold out the replacement stock in a week, because it turns out the sentence, *they pulled it themselves before anyone made them* is, in the salon telegraph, indistinguishable from advertising.

* *

The laboratory report landed the following Monday, and it read the way the noses had said it would.

The suspect lot sat outside the agreed specification on two parameters. The cause traced in one afternoon, because Romero's batch records, kept per the agreement, showed it in plain ink: a carrier ingredient's usual grade had gone on backorder mid-run, and Neto, under deadline, had substituted what the supplier swore was an equivalent, same name, adjacent grade, without notice to the client, which the agreement required, and which his own honesty required him to say out loud before anyone found it, and he did, on the call, with his father's hand arriving on his shoulder halfway through the sentence.

"The mistake is mine," Neto said. "The deadline was mine; the call was mine, and the clause I skipped was the one I lobbied my own father to sign. I have no defense. I have a proposal." The proposal was the remedy ladder, executed without a fight: rework what could be reworked, replace the rest at Romero's cost, the laboratory's bill to Romero under the tiebreaker clause, loser pays, and one addition Neto asked to write into his own shop's procedures, a change-control rule, no substitution of anything, ever, without written client approval first, "so that the next deadline argues with a document instead of with me at eleven at night."

Aurelio took the phone at the end, and the old man said one thing, and it closed the file better than any release I could draft. "*Mi socio.* Thirty-four years, and my first blemish arrives, and it arrives with a map, a protocol, and a laboratory, and nobody is screaming, and my son is a better man tonight than this morning. You told me once the paper protects the shop from itself." A pause traveled down from Hialeah. "Send the señora my apology, and tell her the classic runs on my line with my own hands on it until the boy's new rule has teeth."

The whole argument, start to finish, from unsealing to remedy, had consumed eleven days and zero relationships, and I made Camila total the reason, because the reason was the entire chapter. The machine built at a fortress table months earlier, the golden sample, the specifications, the inspection rights, the ladder, the tiebreaker, had decided every question before it could become a fight. "The argument took eleven days," she wrote in the file, "because it had been settled for eight months."

The costs were real and María insisted they be printed, not softened: about nine thousand dollars all-in for the withdrawal after Romero's remedy, a dented growth budget, a gap on four shelves for one week. Against it, Camila's dashboard logged the other column: every stockist retained, two of four increasing orders, a reaction customer converted into what she now called, in the row header, LA SEÑORA DE KENDALL, PERMANENT, and a sentence traveling the telegraph that no budget could have purchased. María read the tally, and then she did the thing I had been waiting all week to watch her do. She took out her own price letter, the one from the uncomfortable afternoon, and found the line she had written to four hundred women, *the laboratory that checks every batch*, and she tapped it twice with one finger.

"The twenty-four dollars kept its word," she said. "That is the whole month, *Licenciado*. The price made a promise, and this week the promise had to stand up in front of everyone, and it stood."

* *

It was almost six on Friday when the intercom on my desk clicked, and Alexa's voice came through it in the tone she reserves for things she had decided not to editorialize about.

" Tío. There's a walk-in at the desk. No appointment." She paused for one beat, the length of a decision. "He says his name is Victor."

CHAPTER NINETEEN
The Pirate's Bill Comes Due

He came in without the tripod.

I had never once seen Victor without a camera pointed at himself, and the absence of it changed him the way removing a uniform changes a soldier. He looked twenty-six, which he was, and tired in the specific way of a man who has been reading his own comments at four in the morning, and he sat down across from me holding a folder the way patients hold test results, and for a moment neither of us said anything, because both of us were remembering a kitchen in this book where he had once explained to a table of people who loved each other that lawyers are brakes.

"Before you open that folder," I said, "two things, because we do them in order here. First, I have checked the map of my own obligations, and nothing I owe anyone else prevents me from sitting on your side of this desk, which is a sentence I am required to be able to say before you tell me a single fact. Second." I slid two pages across to him. "An engagement letter. What I will do, what I will not do, what it costs, what happens if we disagree. Read it. All of it. Out loud if it helps."

Victor looked at the pages, and something crossed his face that I chose not to name for him, because a man arriving at his first real signature deserves privacy on the way there. He read it, completely, moving a finger under the lines like a careful reader, and he signed, and it occurred to me that the first honest paper of Victor's business life was the one hiring the profession he had spent a year calling a tax on momentum.

"Okay," he said quietly. "Here's everything."

The folder held a year of consequences filed in no order, and I read them in the order the law would: a letter from the federal government, dated eleven days earlier, four days of its response clock remaining, itemizing the claims of FuegoGrow and FuegoGrow MAX in the flat prosecutorial style I had once read aloud to two women under a corkboard, except this one had a name in the address block and the name was his. Behind it sat the trademark demand about the word Fuego, which he had performed for forty thousand people and never answered. Behind that, the processor's reserve notices, his revenue in custody, his refund queue compounding. And behind everything, one page, the page, the standard agreement, with Sammy's smiling signature at the bottom, and stapled to it a printout Victor had made himself, side by side photographs, flames and volcano, same bottle, same cap, same fill line.

"He's selling my formula," Victor said, and for one second the old voice tried to come back, the announcement voice, the voice for bullies and Big Pharma. "That's theft, right? That's, like, the clearest theft in the world. You saw the shelf yourself, bro, everyone's seen the photo, eleven thousand shares. So, we sue him. That's why I'm here. Tell me we destroy him."

"Put the folder down, Victor, because before anything else, I owe you the inventory, and the inventory is going to hurt, and the terms of that letter you just signed include my obligation not to sell you a beautiful lawsuit, I know you cannot win. So here is the first hour, and the first hour is silence from you and arithmetic from me, and if you can sit through it without performing, we can build something after. Can you?"

He opened his mouth. He closed it. He nodded, and I will give him this forever: he sat through the whole thing, and it was the hardest sitting I had watched anyone do in that chair all year.

* *

"Start with the theft, because it is the wound you came in with, and because the truth about it governs everything else. For information to be stolen, Victor, it first must be secret, and the law asks two questions about that. Was it not known, and did its owner guard it with reasonable effort? Now walk your own year with me. Fourteen months ago, you filmed yourself mixing the formula, amounts, order, brand names on the bottles, and you published it to two hundred thousand people with the word secret in the title, because process content performs. Your confidentiality program with your factory was, in your own words, a group chat. And the one-page Sammy handed you promises reasonable discretion, defines nothing, forbids him nothing, contains no promise not to use what he learned, and expires, in any case, in two years. So, when you ask me whether Sammy stole your formula, here is the sentence I have been dreading on your behalf since a showroom in this book that you have never read. You were not robbed first, Victor. You were robbed second. The first person to take that formula from you was you, on camera, for engagement, and the law does not build fences around things their owners have already thrown over the wall."

He did not perform. He sat with it, and his jaw worked once, and he stayed silent, which was the assignment.

"Could a lawyer construct a claim anyway? Lawyers can construct anything. Perhaps the launch version differed from the video version by some sliver only Sammy ever saw, and perhaps a court would care. But now hear the economics, because enforcement is a product and it has a price tag. That case runs for two years and something like two hundred thousand dollars against a defendant who will counterclaim for the invoice balance you still owe him, and you would be shopping for that justice with a bank account currently held in custody by your payment processor. Litigation on fumes is not persistence, Victor. It is a second bankruptcy with better lighting. So, the lawsuit goes in a pile I am going to name in a minute, and the pile is not called justice. Now the letter, because the letter has a clock. Four days. The government has read your labels, your site, your captions, and your name, which is itself a claim, because a product called FuegoGrow promises growth every time anyone says it out loud, and the government's position, correctly, is that promises about growth make a bottle a drug, and unapproved drugs may not be sold, and none of this is a debate we are going to have with them, because we would lose, and because you should lose. The path back into the world is narrow and it is real, and it consists of doing everything they want faster than they asked, in writing, with proof. The claims die everywhere, today. The name dies with them." I watched that one land, because a man can absorb losing money faster than losing the word he built. "The remaining stock does not ship. The guarantee gets honored, all of it, which is where your frozen reserve finally becomes useful, because the money your processor is holding exists for exactly this, and refunding five thousand believers is not a punishment, Victor. It is the last true advertisement your old company will ever run."

He raised his hand then, and the old self made its second attempt. "What if we frame the rebrand as a, like, an evolution, a founder's journey, I could do a whole series on—"

"Victor."

"Right." He put the hand down. He breathed. And then, third time, the thing happened that I had been testing for since the engagement letter, the thing the whole meeting was secretly about. He started again, "And for the apology video, I'm thinking we shoot it at—" and he heard himself, alone, unassisted, and stopped, and sat back, and said, in a voice I had not heard from him before, "I'm doing it right now, aren't I. Performing. Even here. Even broke." He looked at the folder. "There's a DM I keep rereading. Guy my age, day ninety, sent me his hairline photos. He wasn't even angry, that's the thing. He just wrote, I believed you, bro. That's the whole message." He rubbed his face with both hands. "Two hundred thousand people, and the only one I can hear is him."

"Then you are ready for the piles," I said, "because that message is the sorting principle, and years ago I signed papers I should have read first, so nothing in this next hour comes from a man who was born knowing better."

* *

I drew three boxes on the legal pad and labeled them, because triage is a discipline, not a mood, and the discipline is deciding what each thing is before deciding what to do about it.

"Pile one, protect, which means the things still alive. Your formula is not in it, and neither is your brand, and I need you to stop reaching for them, because salvage begins with an honest death certificate. What is alive is this. Two hundred thousand people who watched you fail in public and have not all left, which means what they were subscribed to was never really the serum. Your craft, which is genuine, because I have watched you hold a room with a fog machine and a staircase, and attention is a real asset in the hands of someone who stops lying to it. Your name, your face, your future work, everything you make from this day forward, provided that from this day forward it lives behind paper, which brings me to the second pile. Settle, which means the things that end by agreement instead of by war. The trademark demand, conceded, because the name is dying anyway and a fight over a corpse is a hobby. The refunds, honored in full through the reserve. And Sammy." I tapped the printout of the twins. "You cannot sue him into the ground, but you are not walking away naked either, because Sammy made one mistake that has nothing to do with your formula. He put his own letterhead on a certificate that called your regrowth serum lab tested, and that piece of paper sits in your launch video, preserved forever, and it means that the moment the government finishes with you, Sammy's stationery is standing in the blast radius holding a certificate. He knows it or he will when my letter explains it. So, we will not demand justice from Nu-Glo. We will demand quiet: mutual releases, your remaining balance cancelled, your artwork and files returned, and both sides walking away from a fight neither can afford, and he will take it, because pirates are businessmen, and the business case for peace will be printed on his own letterhead. And pile three, let go, and this is the one you will revisit at four in the morning for a year, so hear it in daylight. The formula belongs to the world. You gave it away before anyone could steal it. The brand is a claim with a logo. The sunk money is sunk. And the fantasy where a courtroom hands you back the year, let it go last, but let it go."

Victor looked at the three boxes for a long time. "Nobody's ever going to make a video about pile three," he finally said. "There's no content in letting go. That's probably how I got here." He pulled the pad toward himself and, unprompted, wrote one line under the first box, and turned it around so I could read it. Under PROTECT, in his careful influencer's handwriting, he had written: *the guy from the DM.*

"Then we have a client," I said.

* *

The fifteen days ran like a drill, because narrow paths reward speed and nothing else.

The response went to the government on day fourteen with a corrective inventory attached: every claim removed from every surface, screenshots before and after, the FuegoGrow name retired in writing, remaining stock quarantined with counts, the refund program described with its funding source, and a commitment schedule with dates instead of adjectives. My letter to Nu-Glo went out the same week, one page, which felt fitting, and it did not threaten anything; it merely described, neutrally, the travel plans of a certain certificate, and Sammy's own lawyer called within six days sounding reasonable, and the walkaway signed inside three weeks: releases both directions, eighteen thousand of invoice balance cancelled, files returned, everyone keeping their own wreckage. The refunds moved as the reserve released, five thousand and forty-one of them, and Victor recorded no content about it whatsoever, which I noted in the file the way one notes a fever breaking. And his entity, when we finally autopsied it, turned out to be a limited liability company in roughly the way a costume is a person, one bank account for everything, company and groceries interleaved, and I gave him the wall speech that a family in this book received in a happier chapter, and we began, from zero, the boring reconstruction that boring protection requires.

The apology, when it came, was the last test, and he nearly failed it, because he brought me two cuts.

The first was beautiful: golden hour, music underneath, a slow push-in, contrition with color grading. The second had been shot in one take at his kitchen table in morning light with a phone leaned against a cereal box, and in it he said plainly what was true: the claims were not supported, the name promised something no bottle delivers, the refunds were out, and he was sorry, not to the algorithm, to the specific people who believed him, one of whom he quoted, with permission, by his first name. I told Victor I had no professional opinion between them, that the government required neither, and that the choice of which man to be in public was, for once, entirely outside my scope, and he sat with the two files on his phone in my lobby for ten minutes, and Alexa, who witnessed it from the desk and told me afterward, said he deleted one of them there in the chair, before posting anything, so that the choice could not be unmade at four in the morning.

He posted the cereal box.

The honest ledger, three weeks on, reads like this, because this book does not sell redemption at a discount. He lost a third of his subscribers, and the comment section held every flavor of humanity, and a handful of creators made content about his content, which is the weather of that world. The man from the DM commented four words, *respect for owning it*, and Victor did not reply publicly, and told me he never would, because some accounts stay closed out of respect for the balance. There is no serum today, and no launch on any calendar. He makes videos about hair, which he is genuinely good at, and reviews other people's products with a disclosure block he wrote himself using a laminated card he asked Camila's permission to copy, and whether the long story ends in a comeback or a quiet ordinary living, I decline to predict, because the honest answer is that consequence does not conclude on a schedule, and he knows it, which is the only sense in which he is ahead of where he started.

He stopped at my door on his last scheduled visit, the folder gone, the tripod still absent.

"Can I ask you something off the clock," he said. "The four pages. Reina told me about them once, at the kitchen thing, and I laughed at it. Everybody who comes here writes four pages. Is that real?"

"It is real."

"What do I even own anymore?" He asked it without self-pity, which had taken a year and a wreck. "Like, actually. What would I even write?"

I took a fresh legal pad from the drawer, the way I had taken one for a woman with an amber bottle a long time ago and held it out across the desk.

"That," I said, "is what the pages are for."

CHAPTER TWENTY
Growth Almost Killed Us

The orders tripled in eight weeks, and I want to state plainly what nobody believes until they have experienced it: the tripling was an emergency.

Nothing dramatic caused it. The withdrawal story finished its tour of the salon telegraph and came back as reputation. Rosa's chairs put the amber bottle into zip codes that photograph their bathrooms. The stockists reordered on rhythm, the website compounded, and somewhere in the arithmetic of trust, seven hundred bottles a month became twenty-one hundred, and a company built lovingly around two women and a comadre began, politely, to come apart at every seam that had never been sewn because it had never been needed.

The family did what growing families do, which is hire fast and hire love. Yandel, the son of a choir friend, came on for fulfillment, and Dayana, Luz's niece, came into the kitchen operation, inside the fence, at the tier the fence prescribed, and I will record that the hiring paper, at least, was done correctly from the first day, because the machine existed now and the machine did not care how busy anyone was. Each hire signed an offer letter that said what the job was and what it paid. Each signed the confidentiality tier that matched what their eyes would see, Dayana at her aunt's own level, steps and never amounts, signing at the stove because that had become the family's custom for papers of the kitchen. Each signed a promise not to walk off with the customer list, and an assignment clause so that any process or content an employee invented on the clock belonged to the company that paid for the clock. What nobody signed was a promise never to work elsewhere, because Camila asked and I answered on record: we fence information, not people. A non-compete pressed on an hourly worker is a leash pretending to be a fence, courts squint at them, the government has been squinting harder, and a company whose protection depends on forbidding poor people from earning wages elsewhere has confused intimidation with architecture. And when Camila, drowning in the week, suggested bringing Yandel on as a contractor because the paperwork is easier, she received the other employment sermon, the short one. The law does not care what the paperwork calls a worker. It cares who controls the work, and we controlled every minute of Yandel's, so Yandel was an employee, with withholding and overtime for the packing weekends, because misclassification is the cheapest-looking mistake in American small business and one of the most expensive to be caught keeping.

So, the paper was right. The problem was never the paper. The problem was standing at the center of everything, approving.

And there was a second problem that quarter, which no paper covered, because it was not the family's problem. It was mine, and it arrived out of my own mouth, and I will get to it.

* *

María had become the bottleneck, and like every founder bottleneck in history, she had become it out of virtue.

Every purchase order waited for her signature. Every batch release waited for her nose, which was defensible, and every shipment waited for her review of the packing list, which was not. She routed the deliveries personally. She approved the social posts Camila had already cleared through rules María herself could not recite. Camila, who measures everything, put the truth on one slide: the average order now spent nine hours waiting, not for work, but for one woman's attention, and the woman's attention was being sliced into fragments no thicker than foil. María was back on her phone at two in the morning, and this time it was not view counts, it was approvals, and when Camila raised it, María gave the answer that founders give, the one that sounds unanswerable because it is half true.

"It is not control, mija. It is quality. Everything with my mother's face on it goes out correctly. That is not a bottleneck. That is the whole brand."

I let that stand for the moment, because some sentences can only be argued with by events, and the event was already scheduled. It arrived in two pieces, ten days apart.

The first piece was Dayana, who asked for a meeting, brought her aunt for courage, and resigned with two weeks' notice and her eyes down. A recruiter had called. The warehouse operation of a certain distribution company, the one whose sell sheets had once stood in wire racks, was staffing up behind its twenty-three new shelves, and the offer was four dollars an hour more than the family could match that quarter, and Dayana had a daughter and a car payment, and nobody in the room pretended those were small things. María hugged her. Luz cried and approved simultaneously, which only Luz can do. And then, because the machine existed, the goodbye ran on rails: an exit conversation at my office where I reminded her, kindly and in writing, of the promises that survive employment, the tier that never expires, the customer list that was never hers to carry; a review of the access logs, which showed exactly what the fence had always intended, that Dayana had held steps and schedules and no head; and a letter from me to her new employer, polite as porcelain, enclosing nothing confidential and stating simply that our former employee carries continuing confidentiality obligations of which we trust her new employer will be respectful. That letter has no teeth in it and every tooth behind it. It converts we did not know into you were told, in advance, on file, and any company that later profits from what she knew does so having been handed the map of its own liability.

"So, the fence held," Camila said afterward, and she was right, and she had also missed the lesson coming, because I had missed it too.

The fence held. The formula never left. What left was everything else, and the second piece of the event arrived the following Monday to demonstrate it. Because it turned out that the fulfillment rhythm lived in Dayana's head. The stockist delivery windows lived in Dayana's head, cross-referenced against traffic and blowout schedules in a private calendar of pure competence. The reorder triggers, the box-size logic, the way the church table's inventory rotated against the salon's, all of it had lived in a twenty-six-year-old's memory, unwritten, because writing it down had never been anyone's job, and when the memory drove away to a warehouse in a better-paying county, the company discovered it had amputated a lobe it had never diagrammed. Orders slid. Yandel improvised. María, seeing the slide, did the thing her virtue demanded: she seized every wheel at once, rerouted the week personally at one in the morning, and sent Rosa's Tuesday delivery on a Monday.

It arrived during blowouts.

The note that came back from Coral Gables was two sentences long, formal, gentle, and more devastating than any lawsuit I have defended. *Doña María: the delivery arrived Monday at 11:40. Per our agreement, deliveries are Tuesdays. Even María cannot be everywhere, and that is why we signed papers, ¿no?* María read it at my conference table, twice, and set it down, and looked at it the way she had once looked at a nine-page chain contract, as a mirror with terms.

"I breached Rosa," she said. "The one term she asked for. The woman read every line of our agreement at your table with her finger, she asked for one thing, and I personally, with my own hands, at one in the morning, because I could not let go of a steering wheel, drove through it." She folded her hands. "We fenced the formula, Licenciado, and we forgot to fence the company. The recipe of the business itself, where did it live? In a girl we could not afford to keep and in a woman who does not sleep. Tell me the truth, I am walking around."

"The truth, señora, is that you are confusing being the standard with being the checkpoint. The standard is your mother's, and it lives in specifications, golden samples, laminated cards, and trained noses, and it will outlive all of us precisely because you had the courage to write it down. The checkpoint is just you, tired, at every gate at once, and a checkpoint does not scale; it queues. Here is the question underneath your whole year, and it is the same question in every family company that ever survived its founder. Are you building a company, or starring in one? Because the hero of a small story approves everything and is magnificent and irreplaceable, and the story stays exactly as small as her capacity, forever. A builder does something much harder. A builder writes herself down, hands the wheel to systems she trusts because she built them and accepts that the highest form of quality control is a company that runs correctly while she sleeps." I paused, because the next question was the one I had been carrying for a while, and the room deserved to hear it land. "And señora, while we are telling truths: who else, on this earth, can make the concentrate?"

The kitchen sounds of the office, the air conditioning, the distant copier, had the floor for a moment.

"Nobody," María said.

"We will return to that sentence," I said. "Not today. Today, the company writes itself down."

* *

The second writing-down took three weeks, and it rhymed with the first one on purpose, because I made sure everyone noticed the rhyme.

A year earlier, a formula had come out of three generations of heads and into a fenced document, split, tiered, logged. Now the business did the same. Alexa built the instrument, in the usual way, generic, no client, no facts, and what she delivered was a kit: templates for standard procedures written so a stranger could follow them on a Tuesday, one page per process, who does it, when, what good looks like, what to do when it breaks; an onboarding sequence; role charts with the approvals drawn as lines instead of habits; an exit protocol matching the one we had just run live; and a structure for keeping all of it, tiered like the fence, so that the company's memory would have the same architecture as the company's secret, everything accessible to exactly the eyes that needed it and no others. She stacked the kit on my desk on top of its older siblings, the interview questions, the true-cost calculator, the memo about the boxes nobody reads, and she looked at the pile for a moment with an expression I had not seen on her before, which surprised her.

"Tío. I think I accidentally built a school."

"Nothing about it was accidental," I said. "You have been building it since the morning you called this place paperwork with a costume on. We will talk about what the school becomes. Soon. This family is not done teaching us yet."

Camila took the kit across the wall and made it the company's memory. She and Yandel wrote down the fulfillment rhythm, interviewing Dayana's old texts and their own mistakes. The delivery calendar came out of habit and into a document with Rosa's Tuesday printed in bold. Batch release kept María's nose and gained a second trained nose beside it, Luz's, formally, on the protocol, so that the standard had a successor even where the checkpoint did not. Approval thresholds moved: María's signature retreated to the gates where it was the standard, the concentrate, the golden-sample comparisons, anything touching the fence, and everything else acquired owners with names that were not hers. Camila's dashboard grew a new row, order-to-ship time, and watched it fall from nine hours of waiting to forty minutes of working, and María looked at that number the way she had once looked at four hundred views at two in the morning, except this time the number meant she had been asleep.

"I slept eight hours on Thursday," she reported to me, with the wonder of a woman describing a foreign country. "The company shipped four hundred bottles. Correctly. Without me." She shook her head slowly. "It is a strange grief, Licenciado. To build something with your hands for ten years, and then to discover that the final act of building it is teaching it not to need your hands. Nobody warns the founder that the promotion at the top of the ladder is becoming optional."

"Not optional, señora. Portable. There is a difference, and the difference is the next part of your life."

* *

There was one seam left, and it sat upstream of everything, and it was the oldest one in the company.

Chapters ago I ended an era in a single sentence at a conference table. For nine years the special ingredient had come out of Colombia the way everything in that world comes, in the suitcases of cousins, lovingly and informally, and commercial quantities ended that, and the family built a small formal channel with a broker and entries and duty paid on every kilo. That channel was correct, and it was sized for a woman selling seven hundred bottles a month. At twenty-one hundred it stopped being a channel and became a straw.

They needed a real supplier at commercial volume, importing correctly, at a price that would not eat the margin Camila had spent a year defending.

I want to state my own rule before I violate it, because otherwise I get the benefit of never having had one.

I do not recommend vendors to clients. I have said that sentence in this office more times than any other except ink before batch, and I have meant it every time, and the reason is not modest. It is that the moment my name stands behind a stranger, my client stops examining the stranger and starts resting on my name, and my name has no laboratory, no audited financials, and no idea what that person is like in a bad quarter.

What I told myself at Christmas dinner is that I was not recommending anyone. I introduced two people I liked. There is a paragraph of difference between those two things and no difference whatsoever in the ear of the person receiving them.

His name was Efraín Bustos. He had been a client of mine for fourteen years, a botanical importer working out of a warehouse near the river, formal in every way a man in that trade can be formal, entries clean, duty paid, brokers who returned his calls on Sundays. He is the only client I have ever had who brought me a bag of coffee every December, unroasted, in a paper sack with the name of the farm written on it in pencil. He was standing eight feet from María at that dinner, and I could see the shape of the solution the way you see an answer, and I walked her over.

"Doña María, Efraín. Efraín, Doña María." And then the four words.

"You two should talk."

* *

They talked. They liked each other enormously, which anyone could have predicted, because they are the same person from two coastlines. They talked for eleven weeks, and in all eleven of them nobody called me, and

I want to be exact about why nobody called me. Calling the lawyer would have meant that the thing between them was not friendship.

I know now, from what later had to be reconstructed, roughly how it went. There was a price per kilo. There were a volume and a delivery month and a payment term and a handshake, and Efraín, who does nothing carelessly, financed a container against a purchase order that described the material the way a customs entry describes a material, which is to say as a category.

That was the entire document. A category and a price.

I had spent a year of my life on the difference between those two things. I sat in a room at Meridian for four hours arguing that *conforming products* cannot mean *products meeting our standard tolerances*, because tolerance is a range and a family's product is one specific point inside it. I had built the specification with numbers where numbers exist. I had built the golden sample, sealed, signed across the cap by two women from two buildings, kept in duplicate, and I had staged the signing of it for a photograph and called it, out loud, the entire technology.

I built all of that for the fill.

Nobody ever built it for the input, and the input is the part that makes the product the product.

* *

The drum arrived on a Tuesday, and the machine worked exactly as designed, and that is the only reason this is a chapter about me and not a chapter about a company that died.

The incoming protocol was three months old, written into the binder during the writing-down, and it said what it was supposed to say: nothing enters a batch until it is checked against reference, by the trained noses named on the protocol. María opened the drum in the kitchen with Luz beside her. I was not there. I have heard the next part described twice, once by each of them, and the two descriptions agree.

She smelled it. She said nothing for a while. Then she said the sentence she had said once before, on a Tuesday morning, with a golden sample and a suspect bottle standing side by side on the same counter.

"It is a stranger doing her voice."

It was the correct botanical. It was from the correct country. It had cleared on a clean entry with the duty paid, and any laboratory on earth would have certified it as precisely what the purchase order said it was. It had also been grown in a different part of that country, processed by a different method, and standardized to a different marker, and it was not the material her grandmother had used on a wood stove and it was not the material inside the bottles Rosa's clients had been buying since March.

If it had gone into the batch, every bottle wearing Marta's face would have held a stranger doing her voice, and the company would have shipped it, and nobody would have complained. I want to sit on that for a moment, because it is the whole reason this chapter is in the book. Nobody would have complained. The mark would simply have begun meaning something slightly different than it meant the week before, and then slightly different again, and a trademark is not a logo. It is a promise about sameness, and the only thing a mark is worth is the number of times in a row it has kept that promise. Six weeks later a buyer would arrive to purchase exactly that number, and would call it goodwill, which is the legal name for a decade of a woman being the same.

She did not put it in the batch. She called Efraín.

* *

Here is the part with no villain in it, which is why it could not be solved.

Efraín had delivered what was agreed. He could produce the purchase order, the entry, the certificate, the payment terms, and every one of those documents said the same thing his container said. He had financed the lot against her word. He had turned two other buyers away from it because he had committed it to her. When she told him she could not use it he was not defensive, he was bewildered, and then he was hurt, and then, because he is a serious man, he began to calculate, because a container of a specialty botanical committed to one buyer and refused is a very expensive object to be standing next to in a warehouse near the river.

María had refused what she could not use. She was not going to put a stranger inside her mother's bottle, and she was not going to be talked out of that by arithmetic, which is the entire reason her company was worth anything to anybody.

Both of them were right. That is not a dispute. A dispute has a rule at the bottom of it that somebody broke. This had a hole at the bottom of it. There was no specification, so there was no fact of the matter, and two people who trusted each other were left standing on either side of a void with a container in it, each holding a different version of a conversation, and each of them entirely honest.

They called me the same week. Efraín on Tuesday, María on Thursday. Each of them certain, in the unexamined way of a client who has known his lawyer a long time, that I was theirs.

I declined both.

I want to describe that as procedurally as I can, because it is the only part of this chapter I did correctly. There is no version of it in which I advise either one. I could not take María's side using fourteen years of knowing how Efraín prices a container. I could not take Efraín's side using a year of knowing exactly how that family decides what goes into a bottle. And I could not have stood in the middle either, because a lawyer who mediates between two clients he introduced is not neutral. He is invested, and what he is invested in is the introduction.

So, I wrote the hardest letter of that year. One letter, to both of them, sent the same hour to both addresses so that neither would hear about it before the other. It said that a disagreement had arisen between two clients of this firm; that I represent each of them separately in unrelated matters; that I would not represent either of them in this one; that I would say nothing to either about the other, then or ever; and that each should retain independent counsel immediately. Three names apiece. And no, I will not tell you which of them I would choose.

Then I sat in my office and watched two people I like hire two people I do not know, for more money than I would have charged, to argue about a deal that would have taken me forty minutes to paper if either of them had picked up a telephone in November.

It settled quietly at the end, the way most of them do. The container went into another market at a loss that Efraín absorbed most of and the family absorbed some of. The next supplier cost eleven percent more and took nine weeks to qualify, and Camila ran the batch calendar around the gap with a spreadsheet that has my introduction sitting in it as a delay.

The specification exists now. It runs four pages. It names the region, the method, the marker range, the reference retains, the incoming assay, and the two noses. It is a good document and I wrote it in a single afternoon, and I could have written it in a single afternoon a year earlier, and nobody asked me to, because the only person on earth positioned to see that it was missing was the man holding a glass at a Christmas dinner, saying four words.

* *

Efraín stopped calling.

There was no scene. There is never a scene with a man like that. His matters at this firm concluded in their ordinary course, his renewals went elsewhere, and when I ran into him at a trade lunch in the spring, he was warm, and he asked after my mother by name, and neither of us mentioned any of it. That December no coffee arrived. I noticed it more than I expected to, and I have noticed it every December since.

María never learned any of that, and never will, because Efraín's file is his and mine. The confidentiality that made me useless to both of them in March is the same confidentiality that forbids me, forever, from explaining to one of them why the other went quiet. That is not a loophole in the duty. That is the duty working precisely as designed, on me, and I had spent a year saying that family that a well-built machine does not care how anybody feels about it.

She did notice something, though, and she made one small permanent adjustment, and she made it so gently that it took me until the summer to see it.

Now, whenever I mention any person to her, an insurance agent, a broker, a customs house, anyone at all, she asks the same question, warmly, with no edge on it whatsoever.

"Licenciado. Is this person a client of yours?"

Sometimes the honest answer is that I cannot tell her. And she says *claro*, and writes nothing down, and asks nothing further, and we go on, and there is now a small door in the wall between us that I installed myself, at a party, with a glass in my hand.

* *

Alexa took the whole thing apart on a Friday, from the doorway, in the manner she had developed over that year, which was to arrive already three-quarters of the way to the answer.

"I'm not asking who," she said. "I want the rule. Because I watched you write a letter you hated, and I want to know what it's the rule for."

"Then write it as two sentences and read them back to me."

She was gone twenty minutes. She came back with an index card, which is how her best work has always arrived.

"One. This office does not recommend anybody to anybody. Not a vendor, not an accountant, not a printer, not a nephew. We can tell a client that a person exists. We can tell them how to check the person. We never tell them the person is good, because the second we do, they stop checking and start leaning, and the thing they're leaning on is us." She turned the card over. "Two. If two clients ought to meet, they meet on paper first. Before the introduction, both of them get the same letter. I represent both of you separately. I am not vouching for either of you to the other. I will not represent either of you against the other if this goes wrong. Put your terms in writing before you begin, including what the thing you are buying actually is, and not only what it is called."

"And the reason for the second one."

"Because you can't unring it." She put the card on my desk. "You introduced them as a friend, at a party, and they heard it as a lawyer, in an office. There's no way to be only one of those at a time once people know you. So, you either don't do it at all, or you do it in writing, and the writing isn't really for them. It's so that afterward there's something on paper that says what you were and were not doing."

I read the card twice.

"Put it in the kit," I said. "At the front. Before the interview questions."

"It's not a hiring page, though."

"It is not a hiring page. It is the page that says what this office is not, and every other page in there assumes it." I handed it back. "And Alexa. Someday, in your building, with your name on the door, somebody is going to be standing eight feet from a client of yours at a Christmas dinner, and you are going to see the answer the way you see an answer, and you are going to want to say four words."

"And I will write the letter first."

"You will want very badly not to. It will feel cold and small, and like a document about mistrust between two people who trust you." I capped the pen. "Write it anyway. The letter costs you an evening. The other thing cost me a friend, a client, and a supplier my client needed, and I will never get to explain a single part of it to either of them."

She wrote that down. She has not, to my knowledge, recommended one human being to one client from that day to this one, which at the time I found slightly excessive, and now understand to be simply the rule, kept properly, by somebody who was taught it before it had cost her anything.

* *

The email arrived on the Friday the new systems went fully live, with the timing this family's story has never once resisted.

Camila forwarded it to me flagged in red, and I read it twice before calling anyone, because I recognized the dialect. It came from the corporate development office of a beauty group whose brands occupy a full aisle of every drugstore in America, it was three paragraphs of manners, and it said that they had been following Ambarina with admiration for some time, the authenticity of the brand, the loyalty of its community, the discipline of its operations, and that they would welcome, at the family's convenience, an exploratory conversation.

I noted the date. The company had spent ten years being a woman, a year becoming a machine, and it had taken the wider world exactly five days after the machine switched on to come asking what it cost. Buyers do not purchase heroes, however magnificent. Heroes are mortal and non-transferable. Buyers purchase machines that run while the founder sleeps, and the letter in my hand was, among other things, the market's receipt for everything the hardest chapter of María's year had built.

And somewhere in the diligence to come, a buyer's lawyer would open the raw material file and find four pages naming a region, a method, a marker range, a reference retain, and two trained noses, and he would nod once and move on, and nobody in that data room would ever know that the most valuable document in it was written in an afternoon, in March, too late, by a man who had said four words at a party.

I called her and read her the three paragraphs, and there was a long silence on the line, the kind with a whole family inside it.

"An exploratory conversation," she repeated at last. "Licenciado, in my experience of this story, when a stranger admires something of my mother's, he arrives next with a folder." I could hear her deciding the way she decides, slowly and completely. "Bueno. We have read folders before. Tell them the family will listen." A pause, and then, quieter, the question that opens the last part of every founder's story, the one no system can answer for her. "But before they say a number, Licenciado, somebody in this family has to answer the older question. What is it, exactly, that we would be selling? And to answer that one, I think we finally have to decide what all of this was for."

PART VII
THE LEGACY

CHAPTER TWENTY-ONE
The Offer

The first paper of the acquisition was ours, and I confess I enjoyed that more than a professional should.

Before the exploratory conversation explored anything, before a single number crossed a single table, the corporate development office of the Group, as everyone in the industry called it, received from my office a confidentiality agreement, two pages, bilingual out of habit, and signed it without comment, because serious buyers always do. Somewhere in a lobby a year and a lifetime ago, a woman had nearly handed her inheritance to a stranger for the price of his patience. Now a company with forty brands and a building in three cities signed her paper before learning what her mother's formula smelled like. I put the executed copy in the file next to Osvaldo's original offer, the first exhibit and the latest one, because a firm should keep track of how far its clients have traveled.

The diligence took Camila one weekend, and I want the reason recorded, because it is the quiet triumph of this entire book. A buyer's first request is always the same avalanche: entity records, ownership, contracts, intellectual property, regulatory files, insurance, employment, litigation. For most small companies that request begins a month of archaeology and a season of apologies. Camila built the data room in two days, because everything already existed, filed, signed, and logged: the operating agreement with its clean seventy and thirty, the license from María, the assignments from Paloma and from every employee, the trademark registrations, the patent application, the stockist agreements with their quality clauses, the safety binder, the withdrawal file with its map and its calls and its fourteen-dollar pharmacy receipt. The Group's diligence lawyer, a precise young man who had clearly expected archaeology, reviewed the withdrawal file and said, on a call he did not know I would quote forever, "In eleven years of consumer deals, this is the first time a recall file has been the best document in the room."

"Ten years to build," Camila said. "One weekend to prove."

The number came on a Thursday, at their offices, from a composed and genuinely likable senior vice president named Grace Halloran, and the number was three and a half million dollars.

I watched the family receive it, because that is my job, and I will report what I saw honestly, in keeping with the policy of this book. I saw two women hear a number that ended every money worry their family had ever had, that paid off a guarantee sleeping in a purse, which retired a mother and educated a bloodline, and I saw both of them want it, completely, without shame, the way you want water. Anyone who tells you their family heard such a number and felt only noble reluctance is selling you a worse book than this one. The wanting is not failure. The wanting is the price of the question being real.

Then Camila opened the term sheet and read it the way she had been taught, which is not for what it says.

"Okay," she said slowly, turning pages. "So, first, the shape. This is an asset deal, not an equity deal. They're not buying Restrepo e Hija. They're buying its things: the brand, the contracts, the goodwill, the registrations, the molds, and they leave the shell of the company behind with Mamá and me. Buyers structure it that way to take the treasure and leave the history, the liabilities stay mostly with us. Fine, standard, Profe taught me why. Now the money, because three and a half million is the headline and headlines are marketing. One point four million is cash at closing. Three hundred fifty thousand sits in escrow for eighteen months, which is the deposit they hold against the reps." She looked up at her mother. "Representations and warranties. Promises about the past, with money behind them. We promise the company is what the data room says it is, no hidden debts, no secret lawsuits, the formula is really ours to sell, and if any promise turns out wrong, they pay themselves back out of the escrow. Which, honestly, our reps are clean and our file is perfect, so that part holds no terror. But this part does." She flattened the page. "One point seven five million, half the entire price, is an earn-out. Paid over three years, only if the brand hits revenue targets. Targets achieved by a brand we will no longer control, run by their team, their budget, their priorities, inside a portfolio of forty siblings competing for the same marketing dollars. Mamá, an earn-out is a price held hostage to a future that belongs to somebody else. You do not sell the company and keep the risk. Except in an earn-out, you do exactly that."

"And the pages after the money," I said, "because money is never the whole architecture. What survives the closing, Camila. Read the family what outlives the handshake."

"A non-compete. Five years, all hair care, all of us, the whole family, which ends my career in the only industry I know at age twenty-five. A consulting agreement, Mamá stays three years as, quote, founder and brand ambassador, which means the face on the label keeps working for the label she no longer owns. Confidentiality forever. The reps for eighteen months. And." She paused on the last one, and her voice did the thing it does when arithmetic becomes something else. "Schedule A. The assets conveyed. Line six. All formulas, processes, and trade secrets, including all rights held personally by any founder, to be assigned at closing, free of encumbrances. The license dies at the table, Profe. Abuela goes in the truck."

The room sat with that, and I gave them the only frame that has ever helped anyone at this altitude.

"Nobody in this room needs me to say whether three and a half million dollars is a lot of money. It is. What you need me to say is what it is a price for, so hear the discipline. An exit is not an event, it is a strategy, and every exit is a purchase paid in three currencies at once: money, control, and meaning. A sale maximizes the first, surrenders the second, and puts the third entirely in the buyer's hands. A license trades some money for kept control. Staying independent pays least and keeps most. None of those is the brave one or the cowardly one. The only wrong answer is not to know which currency your family runs on. So, before anyone negotiates a comma, we are going to find out. We are going to ask them three questions, and they are not legal questions, and I will not be the one asking."

* *

María asked her three questions the following week, across the Group's beautiful table, and Grace Halloran, to her permanent credit, answered every one of them honestly, which is how the deal died with everyone's dignity intact.

"In my company," María said, "there is a row in the spreadsheet called LO QUE NO SE COBRA. What is not charged. A woman in Pereira receives a bottle every month and no invoice, and she does not know it, and she never will. Tell me what happens to that row."

Grace considered it like the professional she was. "I can promise you our integration team would hear the story. I cannot promise you a line item survives three annual budget reviews I will not be in the room for. I would be lying if I said otherwise, and I suspect lying ends this meeting."

"It would. Second question. When a batch passes every instrument and fails my nose, who wins?"

"Our quality systems are genuinely excellent, señora. Better instrumented than anything a company your size could afford." A small, honest pause. "The instruments win. That is what standardization means. It is most of why acquisitions like this succeed."

"And in year four," María said, "when a person I will never meet is asked to improve the margin of my mother's formula by forty cents a bottle, what happens?"

"Portfolio pricing discipline happens," Grace said quietly. "Reformulation within consumer-acceptable tolerances. It is on page nine, in different words. Señora, I have done eleven of these. You are asking me whether the things that made your brand worth three and a half million dollars survive the purchase of it, and the honest answer is: the trademark survives. The rest becomes our best efforts."

María nodded slowly, without anger, the way she nods when a shape she has seen before comes around again, and she stood and offered her hand.

"Thank you for not lying to me even once," she said. "You are offering my family three and a half million dollars for a set of promises, and you have just told me, with respect, that the promises are the one thing your company cannot afford. The price was never too low, señorita. The currency was wrong."

The kitchen council that ratified it ran past midnight, because the book you are holding refuses to pretend the vote was easy. The sister in Queens, on speaker, said take the money, said it twice, said her mother crossed a border with a recipe in her memory precisely so that someday somebody could hand this family a wire transfer, and she was not wrong, and everyone at the table let her not be wrong out loud for a while. Luz talked about her knees and about retirement, honestly, and then said that she had signed her promise at a stove, and stoves are not among the assets on Schedule A. Reina cried at both arguments, which is Reina. Camila said the truest thing, which is that she did not want the money because she wanted the job, the whole job, someday, the chair her mother sat in, and a five-year non-compete was a price no one at that table had the right to pay with her future. And María, at the end, said the sentence I have repeated to every founder since.

"My mother was never in her life offered enough money to practice saying no. That is the part of the inheritance she could not leave me. So, we are going to buy it ourselves tonight, with a wire transfer we decline. The company stays. Write the beautiful people a beautiful letter, *Licenciado*. And *mija*, put a copy of the term sheet in my purse."

* *

The Ferraros chose the other door in the same season, and both doors were correct, and holding both truths at once is the entire reason their family is in this book.

Silvia and Diego had reached the question every childless couple with a secret reach, and they reached it the way they did everything, together, on the same side of the desk. Thirty-four years of marriage, the rinse that made gray hair surrender, her recipe, his hands, and behind them no one: no children in the salon, no niece at the stove, no successor for the two heads that slept in one bed. Their fork was the family's fork, exit or independence, and their answer was opposite, and their answer was right, because the currencies ran differently in their house. They did not need control; their knees and their calendars were done with control. They did not need maximum money; they needed income that outlived standing at a sink. What they needed, Silvia said, watching me over her glasses, was for the recipe to be somewhere it would be loved after they could no longer love it themselves, and to pay their light bill from a beach chair while it was.

"A license," I said. "You are describing a license. You keep the ownership. Someone worthy receives the right to make it and sell it, exclusively, under rules you write, and pays you a royalty on every bottle for as long as bottles exist. The recipe gets heirs by contract, señora, and you get a pension from your own grandmother."

"And the worthy someone," Silvia said, in the porteño way, sideways, already knowing. "*Mirá*, we have watched one company in this city pull its own product off the shelves before anyone forced it and call four hundred and eighty women to apologize personally and put a Tuesday in writing because a delivery during blowouts is an insult. Diego and I did not spend thirty-four years building a rinse to leave it with strangers, *viste*. We know whose kitchen we want."

Which brought the ethics of it, and I put the ethics on the table before the romance could blur them, because this book models the profession or it models nothing. Two clients of mine, on two sides of one contract, cannot share one lawyer, no matter how much everyone loves everyone. I said it plainly: I would represent Restrepo e Hija in this negotiation, because they were the company whose whole architecture I had built, and the Ferraros would have their own counsel, chosen freely, and I handed them three names, and Silvia interviewed all three like a woman buying a horse and hired Elena Suárez, and for six weeks Elena and I negotiated against each other on behalf of people who kept trying to feed each other at the meetings.

The license Elena won for them was better than the first draft I sent her, which is the system working. It ran exclusively, worldwide, for as long as the royalties flowed. The rate was six percent of net sales, with a minimum every year whether bottles moved or not, so that the family could never simply park the rinse in a drawer, because a shelved license is a stolen retirement. Quality control came with teeth: Silvia held approval, for her lifetime, over any change to the formula, and a training obligation, written into the contract like a dowry, bound her to spend one year teaching the rinse to the only two noses in Miami she trusted, María's and Luz's, so that the standard would have successors even after the standard-setter retired to her beach chair. Diego's method, his hands, the timing and technique he had perfected over two decades, came written down at last, his own four pages grown into a protocol, licensed alongside the recipe as one inheritance. And the money survives them by design: the royalties run to Silvia and Diego together, then to the survivor, and then where their own papers send them, which is a scholarship in Córdoba for girls who want to study chemistry, because that is what two people build when the law finally asks them what forever should look like.

They signed at my conference table on a Friday, all four chairs full, Elena and I on opposite sides and both families on the same one, and when the last signature dried, Diego, who had spoken perhaps forty words across two years of representation, aligned the pages with the table's edge and delivered his entire philosophy in the register he had used the first day.

"Her recipe. My hands." He tapped the agreement once. "Now, paper."

Two families had faced one fork in one season. The family with an heir declined a fortune to keep their company. The family without one licensed a legacy to fund a beach chair and a scholarship. If you are reading this book for the answer, I am sorry. There are two, and there always were, and the only universal mistake is believing your neighbor's currency is yours.

* *

The Group took the decline with grace, because Grace was who they had sent, and her last email wished the family well and left a door open that I filed without closing. And the whole episode would have ended there, as a chapter about a road not taken, except for one page of the dead deal that refused to die.

It was a diligence question, item forty-one on the Group's checklist, unanswered when the music stopped, and their precise young lawyer had flagged it in the polite italics that lawyers use for live grenades: *Please describe succession arrangements for intellectual property licensed from founder María Restrepo, including disposition upon founder's death or incapacity.*

Camila found it while archiving the data room, and brought it to the Thursday meeting, and read it out loud, and the room went quiet in a way it had not gone quiet for the three and a half million dollars.

"We could not answer it," she said. "Profe. A billion-dollar company asked us what happens to the license, to the formula, to everything, if something happens to Mamá, and the honest answer in the file is nothing. There is no answer. The operating agreement says her membership interest passes on to family. Nobody ever said what happens to the thing the whole company only borrows." She looked at her mother, and then at me. "We just declined a fortune to keep it. Keep it where? In a person? People are not a place, Profe. You taught us that about companies. Nobody taught us that about Mamá."

María sat with her hands folded for a long moment, and when she spoke, she spoke to the amber bottles on the corner of my desk, the named one and the nameless one, the beginning of everything.

"A year ago, I came to this office to ask a smaller question. Whether a paper could take my mother's formula away from me." She turned to me, and her face had the look it gets when she is about to hand me a mountain. "Now I am asking the real one, *Licenciado*, the one underneath all of it. We have decided not to sell it. So, teach us how to keep it. Not for a year. Past me. Past all of us. Show me where a formula lives when the woman it lives in is gone."

"That, señora," I said, "is the last architecture, and we start Monday."

CHAPTER TWENTY-TWO

The Architecture of Keeping

On Monday I turned the whiteboard around, and the first thing I told them was that everything we were about to build would have been built backward if they had taken the money.

"A company built to be sold is organized for conveyance. Everything in one tidy package, every asset gathered where a buyer can lift it with one signature, the whole estate arranged to leave. A company built to be inherited is organized for the opposite purpose. Its treasures are separated from its risks, its ownership is arranged to survive its owners, and its most valuable things are placed where the fewest kinds of disaster can reach them. Last Thursday your family decided which company this is. So, today we stop building a business, señora, and start building the thing that holds one."

I drew three boxes on the whiteboard, stacked like floors of a house, and we spent the morning moving the family's world into them.

The bottom box was the one they already knew, Restrepo e Hija, the operating company, and I told them what it would become: the place where the risk lives, on purpose, and nothing else. The trucks, the inventory, the employees, the stockist contracts, the bank line, the lawsuits that may someday come, all of it stays in the box that touches the world, because touching the world is where lawsuits come from. What leaves the box is everything a lawsuit would love to find there.

The middle box was new, and when I wrote its proposed name on the whiteboard, María went very still, because the name was Martica Holdings, LLC.

"The trademark office refused her name to the shelf," I said, "because a company in New Jersey got there first, and that wound has been sitting in this family's file for a year and a half. But hear the distinction, because it is the same lesson from the day this company was named, standing in a new doorway. A brand name lives in commerce, on labels, in customers' mouths, and there the law asks who was first. A legal name lives in a government filing cabinet, invisible to every shopper on earth, and there the law asks almost nothing. No customer will ever see the vault's name. No bottle will ever wear it. Which means the register that rejected Martica has no jurisdiction over this box, and your mother's name, señora, is available for the one job worthy of it. She could not be the label. She can be the vault."

María looked at the whiteboard for a long moment, and then she said, "Write it," in the voice she uses for final things, and Martica Holdings became the middle box, the holding company, the vault. Into it, by written assignment, recorded where recording is done, would go every crown the family owned: the Ambarina trademarks, the patent application with its metering claims, the copyrights in Paloma's portrait and label, and, at last, leaving the person it had lived in, the formula itself, assigned by a confidential instrument from María to the vault, with the sealed envelopes and the split pages and the logs traveling with it. The old license, the one that had saved the crown from a bank's lien and an angel's condition, would be retired with honors and replaced by a new one running from the vault down to the operating company, market terms, real royalties, papered like strangers, because the day anyone ever questions the architecture, the architecture must look like commerce and not like a shell game.

"And the vault will have two owners," I said, "which is a Florida peculiarity worth one minute of your life. In this state, the wall around a company with a single owner is thinner than the wall around a company with several. A creditor chasing one person can sometimes reach straight through a one-owner box, where a multi-owner box would stop him at the door with a much weaker remedy. The difference is one owner. So, Camila will hold a sliver of the vault directly, real money for a real percentage, documented, and the wall gets its full thickness for the price of doing honestly what we would want to do anyway."

The top box was the one this family had never once discussed, and I wrote its plain name, the trust, and watched the temperature of the room change the way it always changes.

* *

"A trust," I said, before the word could grow fangs, "is a box with rules and a keeper. That is the entire technology, and it is seven hundred years old. You place property in the box. You write the rules for what the box does, in every future you can imagine, including the ones that frighten you. And you name the keeper, the trustee, who must follow the rules, and a successor keeper, and a successor to the successor, so that the box never, under any circumstance, finds itself without hands. Then the box, and not your mortal name, owns the vault. And here is what that buys, señora, in the plainest words I have. When you someday cannot answer the phone, for a week or forever, nothing stops. No court proceeding is required to figure out who owns your empire, because the box owns it and the box does not die. No judge inventories your assets in a public file for every Osvaldo in Florida to read. The successor keeper, whom you chose at this table on a calm Tuesday, simply keeps. The license keeps paying. The royalties to Silvia and Diego keep flowing. The company keeps shipping. Probate, señora, is the government's estate plan for families who never wrote their own, and it is slow, public, and expensive, and your family will never meet it."

"And the keeper after me," María said. It was not a question. She was looking at her daughter.

"Named today, in writing, with powers drafted broad, and I mean deliberately broad, because the one thing I can promise about the future is that it will not match our predictions, and a keeper with narrow powers is a keeper who must ask a court for permission to handle a world nobody foresaw. And one more set of rules goes in the box, and this one is for you, Camila, so listen to the way you listen to numbers. The trust your mother signs will carry what the law calls a spendthrift provision for everyone who ever benefits after her. In ordinary words: what the box holds for you, your worst future day cannot lose. Not a creditor of yours, not a lawsuit against you, not a marriage of yours that ends badly, not even a version of you having a catastrophic year can reach through and take what the box protects, because you will not technically own it. The box will, on your behalf, under rules written by a woman who loved you before your troubles existed. Some people hear that clause as insulting. I invite you to hear it correctly. It is your mother arranging to protect you from every enemy you have not met yet, including, if it ever comes to that, yourself."

Camila was quiet for a moment. "Abuela had a version of that," she finally said. "She just called it *no le cuentes a nadie lo que tienes.*" Do not tell anyone what you have. "You are telling me the law built a machine out of my great-grandmother's advice."

"The law built many machines out of grandmothers' advice. That is most of what the law is. Now, the borders, because this family has never lived in only one country and its architecture cannot either." I gave them the cross-border hour in its plainest form. The little house in Medellín, Marta's house, rented these eleven years to a cousin, does not obey Florida. Colombia has its own succession law, older and stricter than ours, with rules that can force an inheritance to certain heirs no matter what any American paper says, and so the house needs its own plan, drawn by its own lawyer, in its own country, and my license ends at the water, and the finest thing I can do about Medellín is know a good lawyer there and say so out loud. And the future has a toll booth in it: the day Ambarina licenses its brand into Colombia, the day royalties start swimming home across that border, they will be taxed at the bridge, because the two countries have never signed the treaty that lowers such tolls for their neighbors, and a structure designed after that first license costs triple what one designed before it. "We will not build the Latin American floor today," I said. "We will simply pour its foundation where it belongs, which is before the building, not under it."

* *

Now, I must record the five weeks that almost undid all of it, because this book has told the truth about everyone else.

The documents were drafted within ten days. The assignments, the new license, the vault's papers, the trust with its keepers and powers and its grandmother's-advice machine, all of it sat in a folder on my desk, complete, needing only signatures, and María did not come to sign.

She did not refuse. Refusal I could have argued with. She rescheduled, warmly, reasonably, twice. The second Meridian release was three weeks out and needed her nose. Silvia's training year was beginning and Tuesdays were spoken for. The holidays were coming, and you do not sign papers about your own death in the season of *buñuelos.* Have some respect, *Licenciado.* Every reason was true, which is what made them dangerous, because procrastination never once in its history has worn the costume of laziness. It wears the costume of a full calendar, and underneath the costume it is always the same single belief, the most universal belief our species holds: that there will be time.

So, on the fifth Friday I called her, and I did not talk about documents. I gave her the arithmetic, and then I gave her the one sentence about myself that this subject has ever extracted from me.

"Señora, here is what this architecture costs today: legal fees that total less than your bottle molds, no tax, because a woman moving her own property into her own boxes has sold nothing, and no complications, because you have no judgments, no claims, and no creditors circling, which means every wall we build is planning. Now the same architecture, attempted ten years from now, after trouble has already found the family: the transfers get attacked as tricks, because walls built during the storm are called fraud and torn down by judges. The estate goes through the public process, and the public process bills by the estate. And the formula, señora, the formula does what unwritten, untaught knowledge has done in every generation of every family since the beginning: it dies inside the person, on schedule, completely. I have watched families pay ten and twenty times the price of early architecture for the privilege of late archaeology." I paused, because the last part was the only part I had never said to a client. "And I will tell you one thing about your lawyer, and then I will never elaborate on it. I built my own architecture years later than I counseled anyone to build theirs, and the delay had a price, and I paid it. That is all that story needs to be. But when I tell you there will not be time, señora, understand that I am not quoting a treatise."

There was a long silence on the line, with a whole kitchen inside it, and then María said, "Tuesday. Before the *buñuelos.* Bring my mother's pen."

* *

They signed on Tuesday, all of it, in the order architecture requires, and the blue ballpoint did not leave María's hand for forty minutes.

The vault came first, Martica Holdings, two owners, full-thickness wall. Then came the assignments, the marks and the patent and the portrait moving upstairs with their recordings queued, and then the confidential instrument, one page, which moved a seventy-year-old secret out of a mortal woman and into a box with rules, and María signed that one slowly, and nobody hurried her. Then came the new license flowing down to the company that touches the world, with royalties and quality control and all the commerce a skeptic could ever ask to see. Then the insurance layers were adjusted to the new map, the umbrella rose over everything, the certificates re-papered so that each box carried its own shield. And last came the trust, the box at the top, María's rules for every future including the frightening ones, Camila named keeper-after, powers broad as weather, the spendthrift machine humming inside it for a generation that had not yet had its troubles.

When it was done, María capped her mother's pen and looked at the whiteboard, where the three boxes still stood in marker, and she renamed them in her own language, which is how I knew they were finally hers.

"*La casa, la caja fuerte, y el camión,*" she said. The house, the vault, and the truck. "The truck can crash now. The vault does not ride in the truck. And the house knows who inherits the keys." She put the pen in her purse, with the treaties. "My mother owned one notebook and a folding table, *Licenciado*, and when she died, I inherited by memory and by suitcase. Camila inherits by architecture. That is the whole distance this family has traveled, and it fit on one whiteboard."

I want to record that the afternoon deserved to end there, and that I let it, and that letting it was the mistake I saw and permitted.

Because one item on my checklist did not get signed on Tuesday, for the excellent reason that it was not a paper. The last line of the architecture memo, written in my own hand, said: knowledge transfer plan, the concentrate, begin instruction. Paper had moved every right the family owned into boxes that could not die. But a right to a secret is not the secret, and the secret itself, the hands and the nose and the waiting and the *how* of it, still lived where it had lived since Medellín, in one head, belonging now to a trust that could not make so much as one bottle of what it owned. *Who else can make the concentrate? Nobody.* The exchange from the bottleneck month was still standing, now wearing a beautiful structure around it.

María knew it too. At the door, purse on her shoulder, she made the promise with complete sincerity, the way all such promises are made.

"After the second release, *mija* starts learning the kitchen. The real lessons. Everything." She smiled at her daughter, and at me, and at the whiteboard with its three boxes. "The release is in three weeks. There is time."

I wrote the date on the memo, and under it, because a lawyer's file should tell the truth, I wrote: *Architecture complete. Teaching deferred. I let the calendar win.*

There is a sentence in this book that has never once been true, and the family had three weeks to find out which one it was.

CHAPTER TWENTY-THREE
What Happens When I'm Gone

The phone rang at 9:40 on a Tuesday night, eleven days before the second release, and the whole chapter this family had been circling for a year arrived in four words.

"Profe. Mamá. The hospital."

I will tell the medical part quickly, because the family lived it slowly and nobody should have to do both. María had been in the kitchen that evening, alone with the concentrate for release two, when her right hand stopped obeying her and the words in her mouth came out wrong, Spanish and English both failing her at once, and Luz, arriving with the *empanadas* she uses as a pretext for checking on people, found her sitting very straight at the table, gripping her own wrist, trying calmly and unsuccessfully to say her daughter's name. What followed was an ambulance, a terrifying night, and then, across the week, the mercy of the diagnosis: a transient ischemic attack, the small stroke that warns instead of takes. The symptoms dissolved within a day. The fear did not. The doctors spoke of medication and monitoring and changed habits, and of luck, and they used the phrase *warning shot* four separate times, as if the phrase had been prescribed.

Two details from that first night belong in the permanent file.

The first is that Luz, before following the ambulance, turned off every burner, sealed the half-made head of the batch in the refrigerator, wrote the time and the state of the work on a page of the kitchen log, and locked the door, because nine chapters of fence had built a woman who protects the inheritance even while weeping. The second is that at 11:40 that night, at a nurses' station, a twenty-five-year-old opened the folder she had grabbed on the way out of the apartment and handed across a document naming her as her mother's healthcare decision-maker, signed five weeks earlier in blue ballpoint among the papers that traveled with the trust, and the hospital, which had been preparing to explain to a frightened daughter what she was not entitled to know or decide, read it and simply began treating her as what the paper said she was. The first instrument of the architecture to be used in anger was used that night, by Camila, at a counter, and it worked exactly as drawn.

"I signed so many papers that Tuesday," María said later, "and I remember thinking, so much paper for a woman who feels fine. I did not know I was signing the one we would need in five weeks." She looked at her hands. "You were not quoting a treatise."

* *

The week that followed was the most honest audit this company will ever receive, because catastrophe does not read your org chart. It simply pulls the founder out and shows you what stands.

Here is what stood, and I record it with the satisfaction of a builder watching a storm lose. The trust sat silent and solid, and no court, no judge, no public file, and no question of who owned whatever arose, because the boxes owned everything and the boxes do not get sick. The power of attorney walked into the bank on Wednesday morning in Camila's purse and converted a dual-signature problem into a Wednesday. Payroll ran. The systems from the growth chapter carried the operating company without a wobble: orders shipped in forty minutes, Rosa's Tuesday arrived on Tuesday, the batch-release protocol held finished goods to the golden sample under Luz's formally trained nose, and the delivery calendar, which had once lived in a departed employee's head, lived now in a document and cared nothing for anyone's health. For four days, the customers of Ambarina did not know the founder was in a hospital, not because anyone hid it, but because nothing they could see had changed, and I want that sentence to sit in the file next to the memory of a woman approving packing lists at two in the morning. The company she could not stop steering had learned to hold the road, and the week it mattered, it did.

And here is what broke, in order of the pain.

The telephone in the drawer of a hospital nightstand turned out to hold half the company's nervous system. The bank's security codes went to that phone. The business messaging account lived on that phone. The supplier in Medellín, the source, whose identity had moved safely into the vault's sealed envelopes but whose trust had not moved anywhere, dealt with the family by voice, in Spanish, María's voice specifically, and when a cousin's cousin relayed that *la señora* was in the hospital, the supplier did what forty years of surviving in his world had taught him, which is to go quiet and wait to see who calls next and whether he knows her. Camila spent two days locked out of accounts she had every legal right to control, because the law of the architecture and the engineering of a login are different systems, and only one of them had been built.

And the concentrate for release two sat half-made in a refrigerator, behind a lock, owned by a trust, protected by a fence, covered by insurance, and impossible, because the other half of it lived in a head the doctors were imaging for damage. Ingrid, informed with the candor the fortress had earned, moved what she could. "I can hold the line slot ten days," she said. "Day eleven, the schedule rolls, and the release slips six weeks, and I charge you the change fee I would charge anyone, because that is why you trust my other numbers." The question from the bottleneck month, the one wearing the beautiful structure, stood in the hospital hallway now and asked itself out loud, and the answer was still the answer.

"So, this is the lesson," Camila said, in the family waiting area, at some terrible hour, with a systems binder on her knees that contained everything except the thing that mattered. "We did the assets. The vault, the trust, the assignments, everything Abuela owns is immortal now. We did the authority. I signed at the bank, I signed at the hospital, the thresholds and the keepers all worked. And none of it makes one liter of concentrate, because succession was never one project, Profe. It was three, and we finished the two that live on paper, and the one that lives in a person we scheduled for after the release." She closed the binder. "A business that lives in one head is a liability with revenue. I wrote that in my notes months ago. I just never once believed the head would be my mother's."

* *

The room where the choice got made was on the fourth floor, and it smelled like every such room, and María made us wait until the Thursday, when her words were fully hers again, because she refused to have this conversation with a single syllable out of place.

"I am going to say the true thing," she said, "and you will all let me finish, because I have been rehearsing it against the ceiling for three days. The teaching was never delayed by the calendar. I delayed it, and I dressed the delay in releases and Tuesdays and *buñuelos*, and my lawyer, who knew better, was polite to my costume." She looked at me without accusation, stating the record. "Here is why, *mija*, and it is not pretty. Everything else, I shared. The company, the money, the decisions, the name. The kitchen was the last room that was only mine. If nobody else could make it, I was not a founder or a manager or a member of an LLC. I was necessary. The way my mother was necessary. And some part of me believed, without ever saying it, that the day another pair of hands could make the concentrate, I would become what old women become." She smoothed the hospital blanket the way she smooths final things. "Then on Tuesday my own hand stopped obeying me, and my words left, and I lay here and watched my daughter run my life with papers I had signed and systems she had built, and I understood something at three in the morning that I could not have learned any other way. If I had died on that kitchen floor, I would not have died necessary. I would have died selfish, with my mother's inheritance locked inside a body in a drawer. Necessary was never the honor, *mija*. It was the failure wearing the honor's clothes."

Camila was holding her mother's hand by then, and nobody in the room was managing anything.

"So. The scare is the gift, and we will not waste it being sentimental past Friday. Camila." María sat up the way she stands up in meetings. "You are keeper-after of the trust, and now I name what no trust can name. You are the keeper of the kitchen. The whole kitchen. Steps, amounts, sources, the waiting, the *how*, everything my mother put in me, starting Sunday, blinds closed, telephone in the drawer. And we will do it correctly, with a protocol, like everything else in this family now, because your uncle will insist and he will be right." She reached the nightstand, took the small envelope the family had brought her from the apartment, and put it in her daughter's hand, and it held the second key to the safe-deposit box, and it weighed nothing and everything. "Also, since I have watched paper defeat every disaster in this book except the one inside my own skull, tell Alexa the family would like whatever she is building next."

* *

What Alexa was building next was, as usual, generic, and named with her gift, and it was called THE PHONE TEST.

I had assigned it from the hospital parking garage on the second night, in a voice message I did not fully compose before sending, and she had built it in six days: a template for any family company, one drill and one envelope. The drill was a single cruel question, run annually like a fire alarm. Take the most important phone in your company and imagine it does not answer for a week; now write down, in order, everything that breaks. The envelope was the answer converted into architecture: every credential escrowed where a successor can lawfully reach it, the security codes married to more than one device, a first-seventy-two-hours card naming who calls the factory, the bank, the insurer, the counsel, and the suppliers, in what order, saying what; a signing-authority map; and, on the last page, the instrument she was proudest of, a table titled THINGS ONLY ONE PERSON KNOWS, with three columns: the thing, the person, and the date by which it will be true of two people. "The table is the whole kit," she said, dropping it on my desk. "Everything above it is logistics. The table is the actual mortality audit, and every family business in Miami will fill in column one, feel sick, and finally schedule column three."

Camila took the template across the wall and filled it in for the company inside a week, and the Medellín supplier got his call from María herself, recovered, from her own kitchen, introducing the voice of her daughter the way treaties are introduced, and the phone in the drawer became three phones and an escrow, and release two shipped four days late, inside Ingrid's window, because the first lesson of the apprenticeship was taught early, under doctor's orders, with María seated on a stool directing and Camila's hands doing every motion of the work, which is how the deadline that had been the excuse for deferring the teaching became, in the end, the teaching's first classroom. The graduation protocol went into the fence documents the same week, written like everything else this family now writes: Camila would make three batches, months apart, blind-judged against the golden sample by the two trained noses in the family, and on the day the third batch passed, the company would formally have what it had never had, a second head, and the sentence from the bottleneck month would die, at last, of natural causes.

Alexa watched all of it from her side of the wall, and on the Friday she came into my office, sat down without being invited, which is her way of marking importance, and turned the whole chapter on its author.

"So, the kit works," she said. "María filled in her table. Column one, the concentrate. Column two, María. Column three, a date." She let a beat pass. " Tío. Do yours."

"Mine."

"Your table. This firm. Twenty years of clients whose whole architecture lives in your head. The family's file, Carlos's file, the Ferraros, Juliana, Rosa, Victor, every fence you have ever built and every reason you built it that way. Column one is enormous, and column two says Ruben, Ruben, Ruben, all the way down." She stood up and put one of her templates on my desk, on top of the pile of her instruments, the interview kit, the calculator, the box memo, the school. "You made a woman in a hospital bed do this. I watched you teach twenty families that a business living in one head is a liability with revenue. Physician, Tío." She stopped at the door but did not soften it. "Column three needs a date."

I sat with the template for a long time after she left, because she was right, and because being right in this office is a thing I have taught people to be at me.

That night I took a fresh legal pad home, the way I have handed one across the desk to every family in this book, and I did the thing the mocker did and the maker did and the childless couple did and even, at the end, the pirate's client did. I wrote my four pages. I wrote down what the firm knows, and who has trusted us with what, and what I make that nobody else can yet make. And the fourth page, the one that asks the question this whole chapter exists to ask, sat blank in front of me for a long while, because the fourth page asks who should hold it next.

I wrote one name, and it was not a lawyer's, not yet.

Then I turned off the light, and the next morning I began the last apprenticeship in this book, which was my own.

CHAPTER TWENTY-FOUR
The Apprenticeship

The inquiry that started the last handoff of this book arrived on letterhead, from the community college's small-business institute, and it was addressed, correctly, to the wrong person.

It was addressed to me. Dr. Amara Osei, who ran the institute, had spent a season watching photocopies migrate through her students' families, a laminated card about the rules of the voice, a one-page calculator with a column called THE HOURS NOBODY BILLS, a memo about what the box says, a drill called THE PHONE TEST, and she had traced them, the way good administrators trace things, back to a law office in Doral, and she wanted a meeting about, as her letter put it, acquiring the curriculum for institutional use.

I read the letter twice and then I walked it to the front desk and set it down in front of the person who owned what it wanted to buy.

"They wrote to you," Alexa said, reading it.

"They wrote to the sign on the door. Every instrument in that letter came off your desk. So here is how the firm will handle the meeting. You will handle it. I will attend, because you are twenty years old and they should see that the sign on the door stands behind you, but I will attend the way furniture attends. I will not speak. Whatever gets agreed in that room, you will have agreed it, and whatever gets lost, you will have lost it, with real stakes, because there is no other kind of apprenticeship and there never has been." I tapped the letter. "You have watched every family in this practice sit on the selling side of a table for a year and a half. Now find out what you learned."

She prepared for nine days, and I recorded the shape of the preparation because the preparation, as always, was the negotiation. She wrote her limits before her hopes, on one page, in the calm: the terms she would rather walk away over, the signal she would give herself, the alternative behind the door, which she built by confirming, with two phone calls, that a second institution across the county had photocopies circulating too. She requested the college's standard program agreement in advance, because she had learned in this office that forms are written for the person who signs on the first date, and she read it the way she reads everything now, for what it is preparing to say later, and on the second-to-last page she found it, the clause she had been hunting since a certain memo about checkboxes, and she highlighted it in the yellow of a woman finding exactly what she expected: *all materials developed or adapted in connection with the program shall become the property of the College.*

"Section nine," she said, showing me. "There's always a section nine."

* *

The meeting ran fifty minutes, and I have sat through trials that cost me less discipline.

Dr. Osei was good, which made it a real exam. She praised the instruments with specificity, which is the flattery that works on builders, and then she made her offer, which was serious and institutional: twelve thousand dollars, one payment, for the curriculum outright, the college's name on the materials, the college's instructors delivering it, everything clean and owned and absorbed, because, as she explained with genuine warmth, procurement prefers ownership, accreditation prefers control, and this was, she hoped Alexa understood, a generous number for photocopies.

I watched my niece absorb the word *photocopies* without a flicker, and I confess my pad already had a number on it.

"It is a generous number for photocopies," Alexa said. "It is a very low number for a school. So, let me tell you what I think you are actually buying, and then what is actually for sale, because they are different, and the difference is the meeting. What you are buying is not five documents. It is the reason five documents work: they came out of real families' disasters, they are taught in two languages by someone who watched the disasters from a front desk, and they carry the credibility of the community that photocopied them to you for free. That credibility is not assignable, Doctor. It is the one asset in this room that dies at the exact moment it is sold. Which is why the curriculum is not for sale." She let that sit for precisely one beat. "It is available."

The impasse arrived on schedule. Ownership or nothing, Dr. Osei said, with the regret of a person quoting her own procurement office; a license would take a committee, the committee would take a semester, and her budget expired before the committee convened. And this was the moment. I knew what the moment called for, because I had trained the room myself: the walk. The capped pen, the warm thanks, the door made real by the alternative across the county. My pad said, in numbers she could read upside down, because I had written them large on purpose: 15K, FIRM. I turned it toward her, one inch, furniture shifting in a breeze.

Alexa read my pad. Then she looked back at Dr. Osei and did the thing I would not have done.

"Keep your twelve thousand dollars," she said. "The community license is free."

Dr. Osei blinked. I did not, because furniture does not, but it cost me.

"Here are the terms, and they are not negotiable, and none of them is money. The college receives a license, royalty-free, renewed yearly, for community and nonprofit education in this county. Not ownership, a license, and my one-page license, not your section nine, which dies today. The materials keep their names and carry one credit line on every page, which I will show you, it is small and permanent. Nothing gets edited, translated, or adapted without written approval, because a curriculum that anyone can rebottle stops being a standard, and you of all people run an institution that lives on standards. I teach the first three cohorts personally, at your standard instructor rate, and I certify who teaches after me. You share the enrollment data and the outcomes, because the school improves or it dies. And the license is for your field only. Community, nonprofit, this county. Everything else, corporate training, sponsored programs, other markets, other counties, stays home with the builder.

You get the mission for free, Doctor, forever, starting Monday if you want it. I keep the school."

There was a silence of a particular quality that I have spent twenty years learning to hear, the silence of a form being abandoned. Dr. Osei looked at the one-page license Alexa slid across, read all of it, which took ninety seconds because it was built to, and then she laughed, once, the laugh of an administrator who has just watched a semester of committees evaporate.

"Procurement cannot argue with free," she said. "That is the one number that needs no committee." She signed at the bottom, and then she looked at my niece with the expression educators reserve for the ones who worry about them in the good way. "Who taught you to negotiate like that?"

"Everyone who ever sat in our lobby," Alexa said.

* *

Now the part of this chapter that the structural honesty of this book requires is the record of me being wrong.

I debriefed her that evening the way we debrief everything, and I opened with the confession, because a teacher who cannot say it out loud is finished as a teacher. "My pad said fifteen thousand, firm, and my pad was wrong, and I want to walk through why, because I could not see it in the room and you could. I would have priced it. I spent a year and a half teaching this office that unpriced labor is the disease of every family business in Miami, that your own grandmother donated eleven dollars a flan to a church bazaar for thirty years, and I sat in that room watching a twenty-year-old give away a curriculum for zero dollars and it took everything I had not to cough. So, teach me. Why does the zero work?"

"Because you taught the flan lesson wrong side out, Tío, and so did I, until about day six of the prep." She pulled her chair up close, which is what she does when the answer matters more than the question. "Abuela's mistake was never the low price. It was that she gave away the *value* and kept nothing: no name on the flan, no rights, no pipeline, no future. The price was just the visible symptom. María's spreadsheet has a row called LO QUE NO SE COBRA, and it is the strongest row in the company, and it is not charity and it is not a discount. It is generosity with a fence around it: one bottle, one recipient, chosen on purpose, forever, and the choosing is power. So, I did the same thing on an institutional scale. The fee was the smallest asset in that room. If I had taken your fifteen thousand, I would have won a number and spent the school: their name creeps into my materials, their instructors drift from the standard, and in three years it is their program with my ghost in it. Instead, the mission field gets the zero, fenced, and the zero buys me things no fee could: three hundred families a year meeting the standard with my name on every page, outcome data, certified teachers, and every commercial field on earth reserved. Watch what the reserved fields do now that the free field exists." She shrugged, and then she gave me the sentence I have been quoted ever since at conferences where nobody knows a twenty-year-old said it. "You taught me that every dollar has a price, Tío. Nobody ever finishes the lesson. Every zero has a price too, and if you fence it right, somebody else pays it."

She was correct within nineteen days. The first cohort filled in seventy-two hours with a waiting list. The second institution called, exactly as the alternative behind the door predicted, and accepted the same one-page license before the meeting finished its coffee. And a regional bank's community-affairs office, having encountered the materials at the college, inquired about sponsoring a branded corporate version, which sat squarely inside the reserved fields, and which opened, when it closed months later, at a number that made my fifteen thousand look like what it had always been, which is a lawyer pricing a school as if it were photocopies.

I put a note in the firm's own file, in my own hand, because a file should tell the truth about its author: *A.'s call. Not mine. It worked because she understood the client families better than I did: the strongest asset in every one of them was generosity, and the whole practice of this office was never teaching them to stop giving. It was teaching them to fence what they give. She finished my sentence.*

* *

The client family's handoff ran the same season, in parallel, and it ran on instruments with older names.

The first family council of Restrepo e Hija convened on a Sunday at María's kitchen table, under a written charter one page long, and the charter would have made Marta nod: everyone speaks once before anyone speaks twice; food is required; telephones sleep in the basket; what is said at the table stays at the table, and what is decided goes in Reina's minutes; and the council advises, always and only, because the trustee decides and the operating agreement governs, and a family that confuses its voices with its votes is a family one bad Sunday from a courtroom. Luz holds a seat with no ownership at all, which is the point: the council is where the company's conscience outvotes its cap table over *sancocho*. The sister attends from Queens on a propped-up tablet and is developing, per the minutes, strong views on packaging.

The council's first season ratified, and the office then executed, the governance the succession needed. The buy-sell provisions from the company's birth grew a funding source, insurance, so that the promise to buy out an interest has money attached on the exact day the promise matters. Ownership and control were formally divided into their two different things, economics and votes, so that Camila's stake could grow now while the manager's chair transferred on merit, and the amendment that accomplished it contains my favorite sentence I have ever drafted, which ties the transfer of management not to a birthday or a death but to a certification: the chair moves on the day the third blind batch passes the noses. It is succession by conduct, in a signing instrument, enforceable, with the golden sample as the constitution's referee.

And María wrote her stewardship letter. It is not a legal document, and that is its power: a letter of wishes, traveling with the trust, binding nobody and instructing everyone, in her own hand, in two languages, about what the legal documents are *for*. She sealed it into the trust file without showing us most of it, but she read two rules aloud to the first council, as a founding gift, and Reina put them in the minutes verbatim.

"Rule one: the nose outranks the instruments, and when the day comes that no nose in this family can tell, hire one, because the standard is the inheritance, not the equipment. Rule two: the row that is not charged is not charity and it is never to be optimized. It is the company remembering where it was born."

Camila's own room came in the same weeks. The annual Meridian terms for release three were negotiated by her, alone, with her mother informed afterward rather than consulted before, and she came back with the volume break María had never thought to request, because María negotiated with Ingrid as a grateful survivor and Camila negotiated with her as a customer with alternatives, and both were correct in their seasons, and only one of them is twenty-five. And in late spring, on a Sunday with the blinds closed, an unmarked glass was set before the two trained noses of the family, and the first of the three batches passed, blind, both judges, and Camila did not celebrate, because the protocol says three, but María went out to the balcony alone for a while, and when she came back in she was calm in a way I had not seen on her before, and what she said, she said to Luz, quietly, and Luz repeated it to me later because some sentences should not stay in a kitchen.

"It smells like my mother is still alive," she said. "And I did not make it. *Licenciado* was right about the last job. You spend thirty years becoming necessary, and then, if you are very lucky and very stubborn, you spend three becoming a witness."

* *

Alexa stayed late on the Friday the bank inquiry arrived, drafting her reply at the front desk she had long outgrown, and when she finished she came and stood in my doorway with the stillness she gets when she has decided something and is choosing the words after the decision.

" Tío. The amber bottle. The one on your shelf with no label, the original, from the first day." She nodded at it, standing where it had stood through every chapter, beside its named twin and the golden sample and the little museum of decided arguments. "When all of this is finished, whatever finished means. I want it."

I looked at the bottle, and at her, and I thought about a fourth page in a drawer at my house with one name on it, and I did not tell her about the page, because the last chapter of a book belongs to its own voice and I had already decided whose voice that was.

"It is not mine to give," I said. "It is the señora's. But I will tell you what I would tell any client who asked me for an inheritance." I turned back to my work, so that she would have to carry the sentence out of the room herself. "Build the desk it belongs on and then ask."

CHAPTER TWENTY-FIVE
Let's Start

My uncle wrote everything you've read so far. Then he came to the front desk on a Friday with a manila folder and a fresh legal pad and said the ending was above his pay grade, and went back into his office, and closed the door, which is the most dramatic thing he's done in two years.

So, the last chapter is mine. I'm going to write it the way I talk, because he says that's the whole point of it being mine, and I'm going to start with my credentials, which are these: for two years I had the best seat in this entire story, and nobody noticed, because the seat was the front desk. I never sat in a client meeting. I never read one client file. I signed a confidentiality agreement on my first morning, before coffee, and I've kept it, and I'll keep it forever, so everything I know, I know the way the community knows it, from lobbies and launches and salon chairs and the mail I open and the things people say out loud on their way in and out of a lawyer's office when their lives are changing. It turns out that's enough to watch a whole world get built. Some jobs come with a window. Mine came in the lobby.

On my desk right now there's an amber bottle.

If you've read this far, you know the bottle. It's the one a woman set down on my uncle's desk two years ago while apologizing for it. *Es solo una receta de mi mamá.* It sat on his shelf through everything, unlabeled, next to the golden sample and the other decided arguments, catching the light like the thing in a museum they build the alarms around, which is his line, and it's a good line, and he can have it back now.

Last month I asked for the bottle, and he told me it wasn't his to give, which was correct, and told me to build the desk it belonged to first, which was homework, because everything in that office is homework. So, I built the desk. It's not much of a desk. It sits in a small office the college gave us, and on Tuesday nights it faces a church hall and a program I run called La Mesa, which we searched before we loved, house rules, and which I filed for in my own name, my first application, my first government receipt, and if you had told me two years ago that a receipt could make a person cry a little in a parking lot, I would have laughed at you, and I would have been twenty, and I would have been wrong about almost everything.

The señora came to the second class. She sat in the back like a spy, which fooled no one, because half the room had bought her product at a folding table at some point in their lives. Afterward she stayed while I stacked chairs, and she took the bottle out of her purse, the bottle, the original, and I watched her press a label onto it with her two thumbs, slowly, the way her family presses important things. It was one of the crooked ones. If you know, you know: the launch run, the sixty labels that went on by hand at two degrees of tilt, proof of human hands. She'd kept one. Of course she'd kept one. And the label has the little circle-R on it now, because the government finally finished agreeing that the name belongs to them, three generations late, and right on time.

"It held the formula exactly once," she told me, "for one afternoon, eleven years ago. Since then, it has been empty, and the empty bottle taught this family more than all the full ones we ever sold." She put it in my hands. "So, the full bottles stay with us, *mija*. The empty one is yours. Fill it with whatever your family turns out to make."

That's what's on my desk. Labeled. Trademarked. Owned. Empty on purpose.

* *

Here's what I thought this book was about, for about the first six chapters: paperwork with a costume on. I said that out loud, week one, to a licensed attorney, in his own lobby, and he wrote it down, because that office writes everything down, which should have been my first clue about what was happening to me.

There's a famous proverb about a man and a fish that my uncle spent two years refusing to quote, because he has a whole rule about borrowed wisdom, and I'm not going to quote it either, partly out of respect and partly because it undersells what that office does. Nobody taught me to fish. They made me build the rod, cost out the bait with my own grandmother's flan, read the fine print on the water rights, check who else had licensed the lake, and sign my name to the whole thing before I ever touched the line. And they did it without ever once letting me inside a client meeting, which I resented for about a month and now understand completely, because it forced every single lesson to arrive the only way lessons keep: generic, mine, built with my own hands, tested on my own family, useful to anyone. The interview questions. The calculator with the column about the hours nobody bills. The memo about what the box says. The kit for when the most important phone in a company stops answering. I thought I was doing assignments. I was doing an apprenticeship, and the thing I was apprenticed to wasn't law. It was judgment. Nobody in this book was ever just going to leave me money, or a company, or even a job. I was being taught to think, to build, to protect what I build, to recover when it breaks, and to hand it to somebody else on purpose instead of by accident. That's the inheritance. It fit in the lobby. It'll fit in yours.

And in case you think this only works for people whose grandmothers left them a formula, let me give you the tour of what I could see from the front desk, which is to say what the whole community can see.

There's a man from Valencia whose sales bar is on shelves in three counties now, with his own impossible last name on the label, and nothing anywhere on the package that tells you how it's made, which is exactly, precisely the point. There's a couple from Buenos Aires who mailed our office a postcard last month, a beach, absurdly blue, with one word on the back in Silvia's handwriting: *Cobrando.* Collecting. There's a woman from São Paulo whose new cards carry one quiet word her old cards never earned, *gentler*, and when I asked her at her relaunch how she could say it, she said, "*Querida*, four hundred pages in a binder," and looked happier about the binder than the party. There's a salon in Coral Gables with a framed registration certificate behind the register and deliveries that come on Tuesdays, only ever Tuesdays. There's a guy with a big channel who makes honest videos about hair now, no serum, no countdown clocks, and who posted about writing four pages of homework from a lawyer he didn't name, and the comments guessed, and he let them.

And there's a family. Their second blind batch passed in August, both noses. The third is scheduled for October, and on the day it passes, a chair changes hands, because they wrote it that way, in a signing instrument, like everything else. Their council meets on Sundays with the phones in a basket, and the minutes exist, and the aunt in Queens has strong views on packaging, and there's a row in a spreadsheet that will never be optimized, and a woman in Pereira who will never know why. Their first class at La Mesa met in a church hall, and we set up on a folding table that somebody repaired one early morning before launch, new wood on the old leg, sanded and stained close, and nobody has ever claimed the work, and my uncle says some signatures aren't for the file, and I've decided he's right, and I've also decided that table holds weight better than anything else in that hall, which is its own kind of signature.

* *

One more thing happened at La Mesa, at the third class, and I almost didn't write it down, and then I remembered whose niece I am.

A woman stayed after everyone left. Late fifties, church clothes, a canvas bag she held with both hands, and she waited until I was stacking the last chairs before she came over and set a jar on the folding table. An ordinary jar, no label, something dark red inside. She turned it a little, so it faced me, and then she apologized for it.

"*Es solo una salsa de mi abuela*," she said. It is only a sauce of my grandmother's. "Thirty years I sell it at the *fiestas*, from a table like this one. My son-in-law says a company wants to buy the recipe, and he says I should be happy, and the paper is at my house, and I have not signed it, and I do not know why I have not signed it." She looked at the jar the way you look at something you are about to give away. "Probably it is nothing, *señorita*. Probably I am wasting your time."

I want you to understand that I heard the whole book arrive in that sentence, every chapter of it, standing in a church hall next to a repaired table, two years after I watched a different woman apologize for a different container in a different room. And I did what the seat I sat in for two years trained me to do, which is that I did not answer a single question she hadn't asked, and I did not touch the paper at her house, and I did not pretend to be anything I am not licensed to be. I pulled out a legal pad, a fresh one, because I keep a stack of them now, and I slid it across the folding table, and I heard my own voice give the assignment that was given in the first chapter of this book, and it fit my mouth like it had been waiting there.

"Before anybody signs anything," I said, "four pages."

There's also a fourth page in my uncle's desk drawer with a name written on it, and he believes the drawer locks, and I believe I haven't decided anything yet, and both of us are comfortable being wrong about one of those. What I know is this: I don't have my formula yet. My bottle is empty on purpose. But I have the rod, and the water rights, and a stack of legal pads, and a folding table that holds weight, and that is more inheritance than most people ever get told they already have.

* *

Two more things, and then it's your turn, because this chapter was never actually about me either.

First, the honest part, in my language instead of a disclaimer's: nothing in this book was advice for your situation, because nobody who wrote it has met your situation. The instruments are free and the principles travel, but the moments when a real, licensed, paid professional mattered are marked all through this story, marked in the clearest way anything can be marked, by what happened to the people who skipped one. When it's your amber bottle on the desk, get your own lawyer, your own accountant, your own chair on your own side of the table. That's not the sales pitch. That's chapter nineteen.

Second, the assignment, because you didn't think you were getting out of the assignment. Everyone who ever walked into that office got the same first homework, the mocker and the maker and the couple and the pirate's client, everyone, and I have watched what those four pages do for people for two years from the best seat in the building, so now it's yours. Get four pages. Paper, tonight, in any language, handwritten, because the hand is slower than the mouth and slower is the point. Page one: everything your family knows, makes, and is trusted for, and be honest, because the list is longer than you think and you have been apologizing for the best thing in it. Page two: who knows it. Every name. Page three: where it has already traveled, everything sold, shown, posted, or explained to anyone, ever, because you cannot protect a thing until you know how much of it is already gone. And page four, the hard one, the one my uncle made a hospital room answer and then made himself answer: who should hold it next. Write a name even if the name scares you. Especially then.

It's late now. The office is quiet, the lobby's dark, and I'm at my not-much-of-a-desk with an empty amber bottle wearing a crooked label, and somewhere in this county tonight, I promise you, somebody is sitting at a kitchen table apologizing for the most valuable thing their family owns. Maybe it's your kitchen. Maybe it's your bottle, or your recipe, or your method, or your grandmother's way of doing a thing that nobody ever wrote down, sitting in one head, waiting for either a fence or a funeral.

Two years ago, the last thing that happened in the first chapter of this book was my uncle telling me to write something down, and the last line said I already was. He thought he was teaching me to take notes.

Write it down. All four pages. I already am.

I can do this. Let's start.

AFTERWORD

Six months later.

The third batch passed in October. Both noses, blind, first try. The chair changed hands the same week, exactly the way the paper said it would, and the señora sat in the second seat at the next council like a woman trying on a coat she had sewn herself and finding, to her suspicion, that it fit. She still runs the batch comparisons. Nobody would dare stop her. The standard was always the inheritance, not the chair.

La Mesa runs two nights a week now, in two languages, and the second institution sent its first certified teacher back to us for review, and I failed her once and passed her the second time, which is how you know the certification is real.

The woman with the jar came back. Four pages, handwritten, in Spanish, and she read the offer at her house against them and did not sign it, and then she hired her own lawyer, which was the entire point, and which had nothing to do with me, which was also the entire point.

The amber bottle is still on my desk. Still empty. I look at it most days and I have stopped being in a hurry about it, because I finally understand what it is. It is not a container waiting for a product. It is a question waiting for its turn.

My uncle still will not tell me what is written on the fourth page in his drawer. He thinks the drawer locks.

We started. That was the whole assignment. Everything else is chapters that have not happened yet.

A.

YOUR FOUR PAGES

Everyone who ever walked into the office in this book received the same first homework, before any advice, before any signature. Now it is yours. Four pages, on paper, handwritten, tonight, in whatever language they arrive, because the hand is slower than the mouth, and slower is the point.

Page One. Everything your family knows, makes, and is trusted for. Be honest. The list is longer than you think, and you have been apologizing for the best thing on it.

Page Two. Who knows it. Every name, family and not, and what each of them knows.

Page Three. Where it has already traveled. Everything ever sold, shown, posted, taught, or explained to anyone, because you cannot protect a thing until you know how much of it is already gone.

Page Four. Who should hold it next. Write a name, even if the name scares you. Especially then.

When the pages are written, do not sign anything. Bring them to a qualified professional you trust, in your own jurisdiction, on your own side of the table.

CONTINUE AT THE TABLE

The instruments in this story, the inventories, the calculators, the checklists, and the conversations behind them, continue where a book cannot: updated, in both languages, at the family table we keep online.

YouTube: @WeareAlcobalaw

www.alcobalaw.com

Nothing there, and nothing here, is legal advice for your situation. When it is your amber bottle on the desk, get your own counsel. That is not the sales pitch. That is chapter nineteen.

ABOUT THE AUTHOR

Ruben Alcoba, Esq., is the founder and managing attorney of Alcoba Law Group, P.A., an international law firm in Doral, Florida, serving entrepreneurial families in patent, trademark, business, asset protection, trust, and immigration law. For more than two decades he has represented founders, inventors, and immigrant families building in the United States, with a practice built on the convictions this book was written to teach: listen to the whole story first, recommend only what is right, and let the client choose the road.

He is an immigrant himself. The torch his mother is passing to him, and the one he intends to pass on, is the reason this book exists.

He wrote it for his niece, one summer, so she would know what he does all day, and why.

Doral, Florida, 2026

ONE LAST PAGE

If any part of this story made you look differently at something your family already owns, there is one thing you can do that costs nothing and matters more than you would think.

Leave a review. Honest, short, whatever you thought.

Reviews are how a book like this one reaches the next person sitting at a kitchen table with a bottle in front of her, apologizing for it.

That is the whole ask.

Thank you for reading.

ALCOBA LAW GROUP, P.A. · DORAL, FLORIDA

www.ingramcontent.com/pod-product-compliance
Lightning Source LLC
LaVergne TN
LVHW022208200926
848481LV00006B/1891